A PHOTOGRAPHER'S
GUIDE TO RAILWAYS

Roger Siviter ARPS

PEERAGE BOOKS

Deltic diesel locomotive No D9015 *Tulyar* pauses in Leeds Central station on 2 April 1966 after working in with a Kings Cross – Leeds train.

This picture illustrates the use of reflected light to bring out the details which would otherwise be lost in an enclosed station. The unseasonable snow seen in the bottom right hand corner of the picture, coupled with the light from the sky reflected in the wet platform, brings out the shadow detail in the locomotive as well as helping to create an atmospheric picture.

From a compositional point of view the diagonal lines give a sense of movement to a static scene and the cab window falls on the Golden Section – see section on composition.

Camera, Konica 35mm range-finder fitted with a 45mm lens. Exposure 1/60th sec at f5·6. Film, Kodak Plus X (125ASA), developed in D 76 (undiluted).

To my wife Christina without whose help none of this would have been possible.

Contents

Introduction

When I first became interested in railways, I used to buy *The Railway Magazine, Trains Illustrated,* etc, and apart from the very interesting and informative articles what really impressed me were the many fine photographs contained inside their covers.

Inspired by these pictures and armed with my first camera – a Purma Special (which has now become something of a collector's item having been the first all-plastic camera) – I set out to try my hand at photographing trains, determined to emulate the photographic names of the day.

The early results were not good and as time went on I soon began to realise that railway photography must surely be one of the most challenging aspects of photography, yet one which can be very enjoyable and at times rewarding.

The essence of railway photography is being able to preserve for ever on film a magic moment that would otherwise, with the passage of time, be a vague memory. The photographic print and slide preserve the past, not only for the photographer but for the countless number of people who enjoy looking at railway pictures. But it is much

The railway scene at night can be very photogenic as witnessed from this study of LNER K1 2–6–0 No 2005 at Carnforth shed on 23 January 1982.

Although there is a natural movement in the group of men at the side of the locomotive, because they are well to the side they do not detract from the main subject. Also note the inclusion of the signalbox on the right hand side which helps to frame the picture.

Camera, Nikon FM (35mm SLR) fitted with 35mm medium wide angle lens. Time exposure of 1 min at f8. Film, Ilford XP1 rated at 400ASA and developed in XP1 chemicals.

more than that, for the photograph is also important from the historical point of view. The invention of photography must rank as one of the most important scientific developments of the last century. We can now *see* the history of the last hundred years or so, a thing that was almost impossible before photography except through sketches and paintings. Until the first photographs were created in the 1850s only the artist was able to record the past and this was not always very accurate. This of course applied equally well to railways.

Although many railway photographs were taken before the turn of the century by some notable pioneers it was not until the early 1900s that the art of railway photography really began to develop through the work of such photographers as T. F. Budden, Rev T. B. Parley, F. E. Mackay and H. Gordon Tidey and later by Maurice Earley, who did so much for this art form and whose splendid GWR pictures were an inspiration to so many of us. Mr Earley was also responsible for the running of the Railway Photographic Society, a postal portfolio club which helped to produce so many excellent photographers.

The earliest photographers used plate cameras, which were extremely heavy and cumbersome to carry around, especially on lineside trips, but which produced prints of fine quality. By the late 1920s and early 30s roll film cameras began to take over making lineside work much more practical and easier. (The famous Rollieflex twin lens reflex camera first appeared in 1928).

Another very important development around that time was the introduction of the 35mm camera by Leica, a camera that could be carried in one's pocket. It was a far cry from the plate cameras used by railway photographers a few years earlier. All this time films were improving to keep pace with the smaller cameras and very good results were possible even with the new 35mm cameras.

Thus in the space of a few years the improvement in cameras, especially in size and weight, and the use of roll film instead of glass plates allowed the railway photographer to get to locations and take photographs which would have been virtually impossible for his predecessors.

By the 1930s railway photography began to be much more pictorial. Until then, fine lineside action photographs, in which the train was all important to the exclusion of almost everything else, were traditional, but photographers, led notably by Eric Treacy, began to incorporate the whole railway scene into the photograph with station shots, shed shots, landscape shots, night shots etc. The 1930s must have been one of the most exciting times on the railways with crack expresses on the four main lines, and the development of large magnificent steam engines and beautiful rolling stock. The Coronation Scot must surely have been a wonderful sight as it stormed up Shap. It is a great pity that some of today's high quality colour films were not available then. However thanks to the efforts of the photographers of the 1930s we do have very many fine monochrome photographs of those halcyon days.

This trend in pictorialism continued until the demise of steam on British Railways when a wave of new photographers led by Colin Gifford started what was to become known as the New Approach. This made artistic use of natural lighting, particularly *contre-jour,* people, reflections, framing the subject and a whole host of new ideas which created a new, exciting and very atmospheric type of railway photograph. This style is very useful when photographing modern traction. Because of the lack of steam etc something needs to be added to create atmosphere. But more of this in a later chapter.

In this *Handbook of Railway Photography* all these varying aspects of photography are discussed, which I hope will encourage people to record today's railway scene on film for to-morrow, since by then it will be history.

I would like to thank the many railway photographers past and present who through their efforts have preserved our railways on film for all of us to enjoy and all railwaymen, professional and amateur, who make it all possible. In particular in connection with the preparation of this book, I would like to express my thanks to Bob Dallow, FRPS, AFIAP for his advice and help, and to Joan Wappett for sterling work at the typewriter.

Selly Oak,   Roger Siviter
Birmingham

1
Choice of Equipment

1) Camera formats

Most photographers must have asked themselves at one time or another 'What format shall I use?' There is never an easy answer to this, as all sizes have advantages and disadvantages. Remember there is no such thing as the perfect camera, but what an individual can do is to find the equipment that is the most suited to his own personal requirements and stick to it. Having settled on the system that suits you and which produces the results that you require it could be a mistake to change. You will find that most of the top professional and amateur photographers have been using the same equipment for years, with consistently good results, which must be a good example for all of us to follow.

With regard to size, I mainly use 35mm single lens reflex cameras and equipment because this suits my requirements, but I do on occasions use larger format cameras as will be seen from some of the photographs in this book. The important point about railway photography is that it is mainly *action* photography, which means that whatever size of equipment we chose to use whether it be large or small format, our cameras must have a shutter speed as fast as 1/250th second at the very least.

We can now consider the main advantages and disadvantages of the different camera formats.

35mm
A very large selection of cameras and lenses is available in this format over a wide price range. This size is excellent for taking colour slides and many 35mm projectors and ancillary equipment are available on the photographic market.

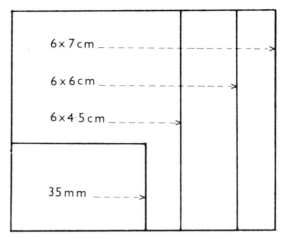

Fig 1 Comparative dimensions of negatives in actual sizes.

Many problems can arise when doing black and white work. In this size it needs a far greater degree of enlargement compared to larger formats and great care must be taken in the development of films. The diagram above shows the different negative sizes from 35mm to 6 x 7cm in comparison to each other, and it will be seen from this the far greater enlargement needed by 35mm compared to say 6 x 6cm (2½in square) to make a reasonable enlargement.

Medium and large formats, 645, 6 x 6cm, 6 x 7cm.
Note:- all these cameras use 120 size film.
These formats are extremely good for black and white work enabling you to use faster films and achieve very fine results.

The 645 system is often called the ideal format with a side/length ratio (6 x 4·5cm) which comes very close to matching standard paper sizes especially in the popular 20·3 x 25·4cm (8in x 10in) paper size. This means less trimming with enlargements which means that the full negative area can be used efficiently and economically.

There is not such a wide selection of cameras, lenses and projectors etc on the market compared with the 35mm size and most of the equipment using 120 size roll film is in the higher price range.

The conclusion that maybe one could draw from this is that the larger formats are best used for monochrome work and 35mm for the colour slides as many photographers already do. But this in turn can create problems, not least of which is financial. Thus it comes to individual tastes and requirements.

One idea which is proving popular amongst railway photographers is to mount two cameras together on a single frame with their shutters linked together for simultaneous monochrome and colour exposures. If you try out this system remember to make sure that the lenses on both cameras are of the equivalent focal lengths. Do not mix the lenses around for example by using a telephoto on one camera and a wide angle on the other as this will cause obvious problems.

With regard to cameras larger than the 6 x 7cm size, although superb results are obtainable with these very large format sizes, some often referred to as press cameras and usually dating from past years, the disadvantages outweigh the advantages for the railway photographer of today and indeed it would only be in huge enlargements that you would be able to see the difference between them and the smaller format, such is the improvement in material and equipment in the smaller sizes in the last two decades.

I have also not referred to the 127 or smaller sizes of camera often taking cassette film because arguably, with one or two exceptions, they are limited in this type of photography, with limited shutter speeds and producing very small colour negatives and prints, fine for family albums.

Once you have decided on the format that you are going to use let us look at the camera types that are available in the various sizes.

(a) Single Lens Reflex (SLR).
This system is particularly suited to action photography and so to railway photography.

Principally this is because the image seen in the camera's viewfinder is the image which passes through the taking lens and is recorded on the film, and it appears the right way up in eye level viewfinders, as on 35mm cameras. But in both the larger format SLR and the twin lens reflex camera (see below) the camera is held at waist level and viewed from above. In this type of viewfinder the image appears as the reverse of the actual scene (although it is recorded the correct way round on the film). On most makes of this type of camera, to rectify this and give the user the convenience of eye level viewfinding (as on 35mm cameras) the waist level viewfinder can be exchanged for an eye level prism.

The other big advantage of the SLR system is that all the lenses are interchangeable, which gives tremendous scope to the composition of pictures.

(b) Twin Lens Reflex (TLR).
The principal of this system is that one lens is used for taking the picture and the other for viewing and focusing, (both lenses are of the same focal length and are coupled together.) These cameras are available only in the 6 x 6cm size (2¼in) and are now only manufactured by a few firms, the most famous being Yashica and Mamiya. A feature of the Mamiya system is that the lenses are interchangeable. The most famous of all twin lens cameras, the Rollieflex, has only ceased production in recent years and many of these fine cameras are still available on the secondhand market.

(c) Viewfinder cameras.
These cameras, at one time available in all the different formats, are now, with one or two exceptions, confined to the 35mm size. Most cameras have fixed lenses, these being popularly known as compacts, because of their compact size, but on some 35mm cameras, namely the famous Leica M series and the Russian Fed and Zorki, the lenses are interchangeable.

Viewing is not through the lens as the SLR system but simply through a viewfinder, usually set above the lens. This means that you do not get on the film exactly what you see in the viewfinder which can be a disadvantage in action photography, and in close-up detail work.

Focusing is either by a rangefinder coupled to the lens and viewfinder or on the less sophisticated models by simply working out the subject distance and setting it on the distance scale on the lens barrel.

One of the main advantages of this type of camera is that unlike the SLR with a return mirror (for viewing), there is less likelihood of any shake being caused after the re-

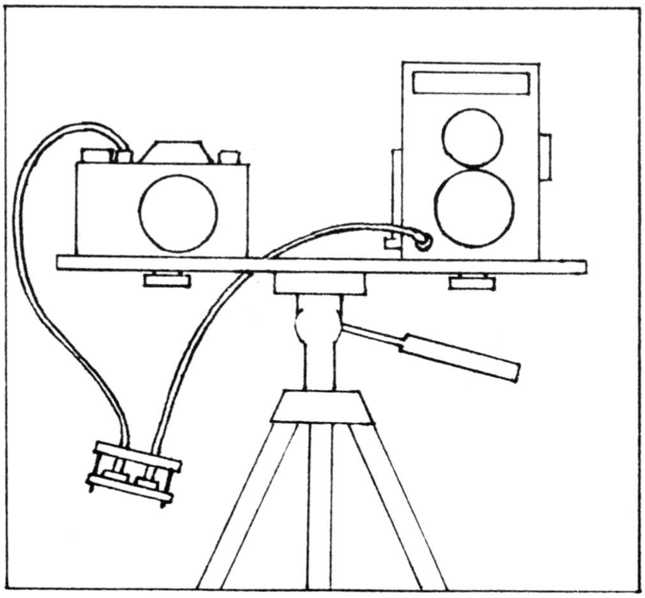

Fig 2 Method of mounting two cameras for taking simultaneous monochrome and colour photographs. The diagram shows two cameras (of different formats) mounted together on a single frame supported by a tripod. A cable release is mounted to each shutter and the two releases clamped together to enable the shutters to be fired simultaneously.

lease of the shutter. But with today's SLR cameras this problem has largely been overcome by improved design of the mirror mechanism.

Summarised below are the numbers of exposures which can be taken with the various camera sizes and film lengths. This is relevant to the choice of equipment discussed above.

35mm
Both black and white negative and colour slide films usually come in 20 and 36 exposure sizes, but colour negative (for prints) can be obtained in 12, 24 and 36 exposure sizes.

645
Black and white 15 and 30 exposures. Colour 15 exposures.

6 x 6cm
Black and white 12 and 24 exposures. Colour 12 exposures.

6 x 7cm
Black and white 10 and 20 exposures. Colour 10 exposures.

The above are commercial film sizes which can be bought at any photographic store.

(Some older cameras giving other formats and exposures on 120 size film occasionally come on to the second-hand market).

Motor drives can be used with all the above formats and on some of the cameras special interchangeable backs can be fitted enabling the camera to shoot up to 250 exposures without having to change films. For this purpose certain film can be bought in bulk length which is then loaded into the interchangeable backs. Bulk lengths of film are generally available only at the more specialist photographic dealers. A point worth noting is that as 35mm film comes loaded in cassettes, these cassettes, once used and empty, can then be loaded from bulk film. This can prove tricky and must be done in a dark room. The alternative is to use a special bulk film loader which usually comes complete with reloadable cassettes.

Having said that, many people still find it more convenient to buy ready loaded cassettes.

2) Films
There are so many different types of film available on the market to-day that space does not permit a detailed description every one; the list below provides a few examples (from slow to fast speed ratings) of both monochrome and colour emulsions.

Films are rated as follows:
Slow – under 100ASA.
Medium – under 400ASA.
Fast – 400ASA and over.
Slow films are very fine grained and sharp, giving high contrast. Medium speed films are the all rounders, combining good sharpness and fine grain with a fast enough speed for the majority of conditions. Fast films have lower contrast than slow and medium speed films and by using certain developers the speed of the film can be increased. This means that the film can be under-exposed (within limits) in poor lighting conditions but can produce good negatives by special developers, a decided advantage in bad weather.

(a) 35mm black and white films.
Ilford Pan F 50ASA. This a fine grain film which can produce excellent results. Also because of its 50ASA speed rating it is quite useful for action photography.
Ilford FP4 and Kodak Plus-X. 125ASA. Both these medium speed films give very good resolution and excellent tonal quality and are ideally suited for railway photography, especially action photography.
Kodak Tri-X 400 ASA. This is a fast film giving good grain and sharpness but needs careful exposure and development to achieve the best results.
Ilford XP1 400ASA. This new high speed film gives results comparable to slower general purpose films and can be uprated if necessary, but it is important to develop to manufacturer's instructions.

(b) 35mm colour reversal film for transparencies. (Processing is included in the various prices of these films except where otherwise stated).
Kodachrome 25 KM135 25ASA. In the photographic world this film is regarded as the finest available; however railway photographers may find it a little too slow for most of their work.
Agfa CT 18 50ASA. An excellent film giving very good colour contrast and resolution.
Kodachrome 64 KR 135 64ASA. Another excellent film giving good contrast and resolution and as with Agfa CT18 fast enough for the majority of railway photography.
Agfa CT21 100ASA. A very good film for action photography but can be a little on the grainy side.
Kodak Ektachrome 200ASA. (Processing extra). A fast film which needs careful exposure for the right results. Make sure the film is processed by Kodak or a reliable colour processor.

(c) 35mm colour negative film.
Kodak Kodacolor II 100 ASA. This excellent colour negative film gives good resolution and contrast and because it is a reasonably fast film is ideal for all types of railway photography.

(d) 120 (Roll film). Black and white film for larger formats.
Ilford FP4. 125ASA. This is arguably the finest medium speed film on the market giving excellent contrast and resolution, coupled with beautiful tonal quality.
Kodak Tri-X. 400ASA. A high speed film ideal for use with the larger format. Excellent for action photography the film having minimal grain and good sharpness.
Ilford HP5. 400ASA. Another excellent high speed film which can be uprated with good results.

(e) 120 (Roll film) colour reversal film for larger formats.
Agfa CT 18. 50ASA. (Process paid). This film gives very good resolution and excellent colour contrast. Although process paid, films are not mounted.

Kodak Ektachrome. 64ASA and 200 ASA. Both these excellent films give good colour contrast and fine grain but obviously the grain is finer with the slower (64ASA) film. Processing is not included in the price, so make sure the film is processed by either Kodak or a reliable colour laboratory. The speed of these films can be uprated but do not forget to tell the processor.

(f) 120 (Roll film). Colour negative film for larger formats.
Kodak Kodacolor II. 100ASA. Good all round film with a fast enough speed for most occasions.

Kodak Kodacolor. 400ASA. Slightly grainier than Kodacolor II but very useful for bad lighting conditions.

3) Supplementary or interchangeable lenses.

Usually on buying a camera it is generally fitted with what is called a standard or normal lens. This would normally mean a lens of between 40mm and 58mm focal length on a 35mm camera, 75mm to 80mm on the 645 and 6 x 6cm sizes and 90mm to 105mm on the 6 x 7cm format.

The focal length of the standard lens produces the most natural perspective image in relation to the picture area. The reason for this is because the angle of vision of the standard lens is the equivalent of the view seen by the average human eye.

If you have chosen a camera system that enables you to use supplementary or interchageable lenses (that is either a single lens reflex, certain makes of twin lens reflex cameras or certain makes of viewfinder cameras) by using lenses of different focal lengths you will be able to vary the angle of vision. In other words if you use a wide angle lens the view is widened and the subject matter is proportionately smaller. If you use a telephoto or long lens the view is narrowed and the subject matter is enlarged. By using a variety of different lens sizes, as many railway photographers do, you can bring ex-

citing new possibilities to your photography. Before discussing in detail the various advantages and disadvantages of wide angle, telephoto and zoom lenses there are two photographic terms which you must understand since they are extremely relevant to this section. The first is 'aperture'. The aperture is the circular opening within a camera lens that controls the amount of light reaching the film. Most apertures are variable, the size of the lens opening being indicated by the f number. The other term is depth of field which is the distance between the nearest and furthest points of the subject which are acceptably sharp. Depth of field can be increased by using small apertures (large f numbers), short focal length lenses (wide angle) or simply by taking the photograph from further away. The depth of field is reduced when using large apertures (small f numbers), telephoto lenses and by photographing subjects as close as is possible.

(a) Wide angle lenses.
When using the more extreme wide angle lenses a certain amount of distortion of the subject is inevitable. This is especially noticeable when taking pictures of static locomotives on shed etc. This because the wider the angle of vision, the flatter the field, which means that the subject nearest to the lens, usually the front end of the locomotive, appears a great deal larger than the subject at the rear of the picture. We can avoid this by using the wide angle lens that is closest to the standard lens on whatever format we are using. With this size of lens it is doubtful if any distortion would be discernable on our pictures even to the experienced and trained eye. Indeed some people use this size of lens as their standard lens.

The advantages of using a medium wide angle lens are numerous. They are excellent for use in confined spaces such as stations and locomotive sheds and are useful when there is more than one locomotive pulling a train and you want to get a good picture of a

double or, as is sometimes the case on enthusiasts' trains, a triple header. Because of the great depth of field given by a wide angle lens they are very suitable for photographing trains on the move when sometimes accurate focusing may be difficult. One very important point to remember is that it is more difficult to compute and manufacture wide angle lenses than telephoto types; if you want good results with a wide angle spend as much as you can afford when buying this lens. The old saying 'you only gets what you pay for' certainly applies to the purchase of these lenses.

Recommended wide angle lens sizes:

Camera format	35mm	645 and 6 x 6cm	6 x 7cm
Lens size	35mm	50/55mm	75mm

(b) Telephoto lenses.
Telephoto or long lenses are the opposite to wide angle lenses. They reduce the depth of field and foreshorten the subject matter. This is not very noticeable on moderate focal length lenses. In the 35mm format an 85mm lens is perhaps more useful than any other telephoto lens, as it brings the subject just that much closer without the 'bunching effect' created by longer telephoto lenses. Couple this with the fast maximum aperture found on this size of lens and you have an excellent combination for action photography.

The most popular of all telephoto lenses is the 135mm in the 35mm format. (See table at end for equivalent lens sizes in the different formats). These lenses usually have a fairly fast maximum aperture of around f2·8 or even faster. This is very useful for action photography (where high shutter speeds are required) and also on dull days when the light is poor. This size of lens is also very good for taking pictures when a train is in an awkward location. For example, when a train is on a bridge or viaduct surrounded by a deep valley (as is so often the case) and you are unable to get near enough to take a picture with a standard lens, by using a 135mm telephoto lens you will bring the

The picture above depicts a scene on the Waterside colliery system on 30 August 1973. It shows Barclay 0–4–0 saddle tank No 19 with a load of coal from Pennyvenie colliery for the washery at Dunaskin. Notice the cloud and smoke effect (which is one of the main features of this picture) which has been heavily emphasised by the use of a yellow filter.

Camera, Nikkormat 35mm SLR fitted with 35mm lens and yellow filter. Exposure 1/500th sec at f5·6. Film, Ilford FP4 rated at 200ASA and developed in Acuspecial.

Opposite is a line drawing of the above scene on which is shown the comparative areas covered by various lens sizes from medium wide angle (whole of the picture) through to long telephoto. The sizes are in 35mm format but in this section comparative lens sizes are described for medium and large formats.

It will be noted that the angles of perspective in receding parallels are markedly different from wide angle to telephoto pictures and that the cropping of photographs does not give the same effect. In telephoto shots the rear three-quarter view of the train is not much lower than the front giving a bunched up appearance, while in standard or wide angle shots the end of the train diminishes in size more naturally.

scene almost three times nearer to you and this will enable you to take a picture that you would otherwise have missed.

The longer telephoto lenses give a terrific effect of compressed power when you take a picture of a train front end on. This is especially so when taking pictures of steam engines. Because of the foreshortening of the subject by the lens the plume of smoke from the locomotive chimney very often appears to rise to the heavens giving the appearance of a volcano on the move. There are two very important points to bear in mind when using telephoto lenses. First always use as high a shutter speed as possible, certainly never less than a 1/250th sec. This is because all telephoto lenses are physically longer than standard or wide angle lenses and are therefore harder to hold steady and more prone to camera shake. Certainly with the very long lenses it is worthwhile to use a pistol grip shutter release or even a tripod and cable release. No doubt in the course of time you will meet people who say they can hand-hold long lenses at shutter speeds of a 1/60th sec, 1/30th sec or even slower. Before believing them you might ask to see their pictures.

The second important point is that because of the shallow depth of field of long lenses, focusing must always be extremely accurate, allowing the fact that however far

away the front of an approaching train may be, the back will be 500ft or so further away if it is almost head on.

Recommended telephoto lens sizes:

	35mm	645 and 6 x 6cm	6 x 7cm
Short	85mm	100 to 135mm	150mm
Medium	135mm	150 to 180mm	200mm
Long	200mm	250 to 300mm	300mm

(c) Zoom lenses.

It is only in recent years that zoom lenses have been manufactured for use with still cameras. They were originally made for use on ciné cameras.

In principal the idea of a zoom lens for a still camera is ideal. To be able to move from one focal length to another without having to change lenses is obviously very useful for railway action photography but in practice there are certain drawbacks. Many zoom lenses have fairly slow maximum apertures which can cause obvious problems. For example when photographing a moving train in poor lighting conditions you require a high shutter speed and therefore a fast maximum aperture.

It is also worth bearing in mind that some zoom lenses are bulky and heavy and again require to be used with high shutter speeds to avoid camera shake. It is very important to note that unless the top quality zoom quality lenses, which are usually expensive (extremely

expensive in the large format sizes), are used, the quality, as a general rule, is not up to the standard of fixed focal length lenses. This may not be too noticeable if your work is mainly confined to taking colour slides for projection but could be a critical factor in monochrome and colour print work where enlarging and cropping is so important. Also, if you are planning on submitting your slides or monochrome prints to publishers for possible reproduction in magazines and books, high quality material is essential, in focus and with good definition.

If you are going to invest in a zoom lens buy the very best you can afford, make sure it is not too heavy and bulky, and also that it has a reasonably fast maximum aperture, so important in railway photography.

There are so many zooms of different focal lengths on the market today that it is difficult to recommend any particular size but try to get a lens that suits your particular needs, one that is comfortable to hold and has an easy action to use.

(d) Lens converters.

Converters extend the focal length of a lens and are for use with cameras with detachable lenses, the converter fitting between the camera body and lens.

As a rule converters come in three different sizes 1½x, 2x or 3x. If you fit them on to your standard lens, say the 50mm of a 35mm camera, the 1½x converter would give you 50 per cent more focal length – 75mm. The 2x would give you double the focal length – 100mm, and the 3x converter would give you three times the focal length – 150mm.

Converters work the same way with lenses of any focal length but the picture quality achieved with them is usually at its best when they are used with lenses of focal lengths between 50mm to 200mm on the 35mm cameras and 75mm to 300mm on the larger formats.

The focusing distance is unaffected by using a lens converter. If the minimum focusing distance is

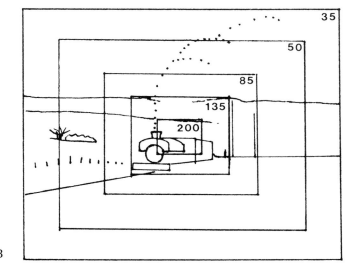

Fig 3

3ft without the converter it is still 3ft with the converter fitted.

There are certain important disadvantages when using a converter. Not only does it multiply the focal length of the lens it also multiplies the f number of the lens. If your lens aperture is set at f2, a 2x converter halves the aperture to f4. This means that as less light is coming into the lens you will need to use a slower shutter speed – half the speed for a 2x – in compensation, which can cause problems, especially in action photography.

Another important disadvantages is that the picture quality achieved with a lens converter is rarely up to the standard of a prime lens. But having said that lens converters are not usually as expensive to buy as new lenses and it can be very convenient to have one tucked away in your camera bag to film that viaduct or bridge scene which is just too far away or not convenient for your range of lenses. Like most things in photography, buy the best you can afford from a reputable manufacturer. If your camera is automatic or has a built-in meter, make sure you can use the converter with the camera's metering system.

4) Motor drives and power winders.

When a motor drive or power winder is fitted to your camera, once you have fired the shutter of the camera the film is automatically wound on by the motor drive or power winder. This means that your eye need never move from the viewfinder when for example you are taking a sequence of action shots, as would be the case if you were winding the film on by hand. You can concentrate completely on the sequence, and you will not miss that vital master shot, as can happen when you take your eye away from the viewfinder, even for a split second.

The motor drive has the added facility for continuous firing of the shutter; this means that you just keep the shutter depressed and it fires off automatically at, for exam-

ple, seven frames in two seconds. However you may prefer to use it just as power winder, and be more selective in choosing when to take your pictures. Naturally you have to be careful not to waste too much film especially when using colour, but it is better to waste one or two frames to get the shot that really pleases you. You might find that in a sequence of around four to six shots you will have two or three potentially good shots, especially the three-quarter rear or going away shot, which is often so easy and convenient to take when using a power winder. Power winders are available for most makes of single lens reflex cameras in all the format sizes. Also, some cameras are now on the market with built in power winders.

Some photographers would argue 'why use a power winder at all?', and, indeed, very many fine action pictures are taken without using one. But they make action photography so much easier and anything that makes railway photography easier is very welcome.

5) Filters.

Filters are useful accessories in both monochrome and colour photography and are sometimes essential to obtain certain effects.

First I will deal with their use in monochrome work. Black and white film does not respond to the various colours in the same way as the human eye and to counteract this we can use various colour filters. An obvious example is when we are taking pictures of trains in landscape settings with blue sky and white clouds. If we photograph the scene without using the appropriate filter fitted to the lens of the camera we will find that on the finished print that the beautiful blue sky and lovely white clouds are not there and that the sky appears to be a white mass. The more we print or burn in the sky at the printing stage the more grain we get on our finished print without ever really getting a good sky so important in a good landscape picture. Thus, in order to get good sky and

cloud effect on negatives, filters correct the colour receptiveness of the monochrome film.

This is obviously very important when taking pictures of steam locomotives at work. To get the very best steam and smoke effects we must use a yellow filter. There is nothing worse than to photograph a steam locomotive hard at work giving off a splendid exhaust to find that (through not using a filter) this has not been reproduced in full on the negative and no amount of burning in at the printing stage can produce the exhaust. Remember when using filters that most of them reduce the light that enters the camera lens and thus lengthen the exposure. For example a yellow filter usually increases the exposure by 2x, which means that you must alter your exposure accordingly by either reducing the shutter speed by half or open up the lens aperture by one stop (which doubles the amount of light through the lens). If you are taking a subject at 1/250th second at f8 and decide to use a yellow filter you must either open the lens aperture by one stop to f5·6 and keep the shutter speed at 1/250th second or decrease the shutter speed to a 1/125th second and keep the aperture at f8. If you do not do one of these two things you will finish up with a thin under-exposed negative which may present difficulties at the printing stage. If your camera is fitted with through the lens metering (TTL) as a great many are today, when a filter is fitted to the lens the meter will take the reduced light into account and give the correct exposure reading making allowances for the filter. But if you have a meter fitted to your camera which does not take a reading through the lens or your camera is not fitted with a meter and you simply use a separate meter, you must remember to take the filter into account in taking a light reading and alter the exposure accordingly. It is worth noting that filters act as very good lens protectors especially against rain or snow or even accidents.

You can use a yellow filter for

Climbing Hatton bank near Warwick on 13 September 1981 is a Class 47 diesel with a northbound passenger train. The whole point of this picture is the remarkable cloud effect which has been dramatised by the use of a yellow filter. If no filter had been used the sky would have been almost white and in consequence the whole scene would have looked very flat. Instead, the sky detail plus the church give an almost Constable-like effect. These sorts of detail are very important in any picture but even more so when photographing modern traction because of the obvious lack of exhaust. Note also the overall rhythm of rounded shapes and the way the bushes echo the shape of the clouds.

This picture also illustrates the usefulness of a short telephoto lens when filming action/landscape pictures. On a lens of this size there is little, if any, distortion or bunching up compared to longer tele lens and by using a lens slightly longer than standard I was able to be far enough back to get a more balanced composition. Had I been any nearer, the balance and composition of the picture would have been considerably altered. When using lenses of this size you still get a reasonable depth of field when working with fairly wide apertures and in this case at f8, a good depth of field.

Camera, Nikon FM with 85mm lens fitted with yellow filter. Exposure 1/500th sec at f8. Film, Ilford XP1 rated at 400ASA and developed in XP1 chemicals.

black and white work all the time, the only exception being when the light is so poor that you need the extra one stop exposure to get a reasonable picture.

Set out below are details of filters that the railway photographer will find useful for black and white.

(a) Ultra violet filter. (Also used for colour photography). Absorbs the ultra violet rays and cuts down on haze and fog. Generally does not alter exposure.

(b) Yellow filter. This filter absorbs the blue wavelengths, making areas of blue sky appear darker. It is ideal in bringing out good contrast between blue skies and clouds and the foreground. Also good for bringing out smoke effects of steam locomotives. Usually increases the exposure by 2x.

(c) Red filter. Has a similar effect as a yellow filter only more so and is ideal for dramatic cloud effects. The only problem is that it usually increases exposure by 4x and in consequence needs a fast film.

Filters are necessary in colour work because colour film does not have the ability to adapt to different light sources as does the human eye. If we are taking a colour photograph on a cloudy but bright day with some blue sky around, the colour balance will tend towards the blue and our subject will have an overall bluish tinge. This also applies when photographing a subject under side or back lighting conditions, for the shadows tend to come out a bluish colour. This is because the shaded areas receive most of their light from the blue sky. To correct this and get the colour balance right we need to use the appropriate filter.

The two most important filters the railway photographer will need to use are firstly the skylight filter. This filter considerably reduces the excessive bluishness that frequently occurs in outdoor colour photography and is ideal for general work.

The other filter of general use is the ultra violet filter (can also be used for monochrome work). This filter cuts out haze and generally makes the picture more distinct; it is essential when photographing near water or in haze.

Exposure is generally not affected by the use of either of these two filters. Too many good slides have been marred because of incorrect colour balance, a thing which can be avoided by using the appropriate filter.

Many special filters are available on the market today, most of which would not be much use in railway photography, but one that could be of use is the polarizing filter. It makes colours appear brighter, clearer and with better contrast and is particularly effective when photographing landscapes with blue skies. The sky will appear extremely blue and could change an ordinary picture into a 'master' shot.

The one problem for railway photographers when using a polarizing filter is that the exposure is increased which may cause problems when photographing trains in action with the slower emulsion colour films.

Last but not least always remember to change to the appropriate filter for whatever film you are using, especially if you have been photographing in black and white and change to colour. It is not unknown for people to shoot off a roll of colour film with a yellow filter still on the lens!

6) Lens hoods.

Lens hoods are very often overlooked by the photographer and yet are such a simple and important accessory. They either screw or clip on to the front of the lens and their main purpose is to shield the lens against direct sunlight thus preventing excessive lens flare when the film is exposed, a thing which has spoilt many a photograph. Naturally they are very useful when taking pictures against the light, and also act as a protector against rain and snow etc.

It is important to have the right size lens hood for whatever lens you are using. A lens hood that is made for a standard lens will not be suitable for use with a wide angle or telephoto lens and in some cases may cause vignetting. This is when the corners of the negative are cut off because the lens hood is not of the correct size. It is thus important to make sure you have the right size hood for the lens you are using. Most lens hoods are made of metal but some are made of rubber and are collapsable. This type of hood can be left permanently around the lens which can be very useful especially, as is sometimes the case, when you are in a hurry to get a particular shot.

7) Tripods.

Tripods are extremely useful for work in places where the light is not very good and you have to use slow shutter speeds (which can cause camera shake if the camera is hand held). This is sometimes the case in a large station with an overall roof but even more so inside locomotive depots or sheds.

Tripods are also very useful for use with very long telephoto lenses which even when used with fairly fast shutter speeds are difficult to hold steadily by hand and camera shake may occur. The camera is mounted on the tripod and the shutter is fired by a cable release. When the camera is on the tripod it can be moved from side to side and up and down by a handle on the top of the tripod. Although the camera is mounted horizontally on the tripod, the tripod head can be swivelled to get the camera into the vertical position if it is required. The three legs of the tripod can be adjusted to obtain the height at which you require the camera to be set.

The main thing to look for when buying a tripod is that it is of fairly sturdy construction that will not collapse and that it is easy to erect and fold away. But at the same time try not to get one that is too heavy, especially if you plan to take it with you on overseas trips. Tripods are also used for time exposures in night photography but more details of this will be found in the chapter on night photography on page 103.

Another two pieces of equipment that the railway photographer might find of use are the monopod and gunpod. The monopod has one adjustable leg which is balanced on a firm surface and held by hand; the shutter is usually fired by cable release. The gunpod fits into the shoulder like a rifle and the camera is mounted on the end of it and the shutter is fired by a trigger on the gunpod connected to the camera. Both these pieces of equipment are useful, especially when using long telephoto lenses.

8) Exposure meters.

Nowadays most cameras, especially in the 35mm format, are fitted with exposure or light meters which work either automatically or manually. An automatic metering system usually has either an aperture priority system or a shutter priority system. Before using any light meter, whether built into your camera or separate, always make sure that the speed of the film you are using (ASA number) has been correctly set on the meter.

With an aperture priority system, set the lens aperture to the aperture you require and the shutter is then automatically set by the meter, and vice versa if it is a shutter priority system. The latter system, where you control the shutter speed, is probably more useful for railway photography, especially for action work where a fast shutter speed (unless you are panning) is essential for good sharp pictures of moving trains. Some cameras are fully automatic, with both aperture and shutter being set by the meter.

But these types of cameras, like the first two, sometimes have a manual override enabling the exposure to be adjusted.

Another system which is probably the most useful for railway photography has the exposure meter built into the camera but is not in any way automatic.

In the case of the single lens reflex camera you point the camera at the subject to be photographed and the meter takes the light reading through the lens. The results are shown in the camera viewfinder which shows whether you have the correct exposure or are under or over exposed (in which case adjustment of the aperture and/or shutter may be necessary until you have the correct exposure).

The manual metering system on a viewfinder camera takes its light reading from a window on the front of the camera which is then transmitted to a dial usually on the top of the camera from where the exposure can be read and the camera adjusted accordingly.

The metering system on the twin lens camera is similar to the viewfinder camera; there is a window or grill on the front of the camera through which the meter takes its reading but it is usually transferred to a dial on the side of the camera from where an exposure reading is obtained. In all these cases you obviously have to point your camera at the subject to be taken to obtain a correct exposure.

The great advantage with the manual system is that it is easy to adjust your exposure when photographing in difficult lighting conditions. An example is when you are photographing against the light (back lighting.) The main subject may be very bright which means that with a shutter speed of 1/500th second the lens aperture needs to be closed down to f11 but the shadow area gives a reading of 1/500th sec at f4, so to get a balanced exposure with some detail in the shadow area an exposure of 1/500th sec at f6·3 or f8 would need to be used. These sort of exposure problems are reasonably easy with a manual camera but could be very tricky with an automatic camera.

Finally if your camera is not fitted with any sort of light meter you can use a separate light meter, a system still favoured by many professional photographers. Simply hold the meter towards the subject, take the reading and transfer it to your camera. Meters though, whether in-built in the camera or separate, need to be used with care to ensure that an extraneous bright light source near to the main subject is not exercising too great an influence on the meter. Equally, darker areas such as track and ballast might influence the meter the other way. Thus it is essential to check the light readings above and below the main subject to assess the overall light range and you must then decide at what level the exposure must be to bring out the detail in the principal part of the subject. Except in low sun, under footplate details of a steam locomotive close too will usually be darker than the boiler top for example.

The problems of exposure and in consequence the correct use of a light meter are well illustrated in these two pictures.

In the top picture, which shows a Brush type 4 diesel No 47478 on a Bristol – Birmingham train passing through Birmingham University station on 8 December 1981, the snow, coupled with the side light, played havoc with the exposure meter and the exposure reading for the whole scene at 1/500th sec was f11 which would have completely underexposed the front end of the locomotive and the shadow areas for which the meter reading was f4·5. With a balance of the two readings and taking the scene at 1/500th sec at f6·3 I was able to produce a negative with good detail in the shadow areas. At the printing stage the overexposed sections were compensated by burning in, and the underexposed by holding back.

Camera, Nikon FM, 85mm lens with yellow filter. Exposure 1/500th sec at f6·3. Film, Ilford XP1 (400ASA), developed in XP1 chemicals.

The bottom picture shows Class 5 4–6–0 No 45042 leaving Llandudno Junction with an evening Holyhead – Broad Street goods on 7 September 1966. The exposure problem in this picture is one of extremely contrasty back lighting. An exposure reading was made for the grass bank on the right leaving the shiny rails to add interest to the black shadows and at the printing stage the highlight areas were burnt in. If a reading had been taken for the shadows and used this would have resulted in a very washed out effect with extreme over-exposure in the highlight regions which would have made it an extremely difficult negative to print.

Camera, Konica range-finder with 45mm lens fitted with yellow filter. Exposure 1/250th sec at f5·6. Film, Kodak Plus X (125ASA), developed in D 76 (undiluted).

2
Monochrome darkroom work

While great pleasure is to be derived from taking photographs, whether it be on the lineside, station or shed, for many people the pleasure of developing the film and printing the negatives is just as great for it is here in the darkroom that you are able to compose and create a little magic. At one time people tended to be put off by the mystique of darkroom work thinking that it was extremely complicated. But to-day with all the modern equipment and techniques this is not the case and can be enjoyed by all.

The darkroom
The essential requirements of any darkroom, whether it be a kitchen, bathroom, bedroom or a permanent room are that it should be light-tight, have good ventilation and heating and have access to running water. Space permitting it is advisable to have both a wet and a dry bench, perhaps on each side of the room. The reason for this is to avoid putting down negatives and papers etc on wet areas, a thing which may cause permanent damage to them.

To process a film we need the following basic equipment in the dark room:
  Developing tank
  Funnel
  Measuring cylinders
  Thermometer
  Timer
  Non-fluffy cloth
The last four items are also used in printing and enlarging plus the following equipment:
  4 developing dishes or trays
  Enlarger complete with lens
  Masking frame
  Safelight
  3 Print forceps or tongs
The most important item of this equipment is the enlarger. Do not skimp on this item but buy the best that you can afford. Make sure the enlarger is well constructed and has a column long enough to enable you to enlarge up to 15in x 12in on the baseboard. It is also very important for the negative holder to hold the film flat during exposure and not scratch the film. Also make sure that the enlarger lens is of good quality, at least as good as that on the camera. So many people have excellent lenses on their cameras but when it comes to enlargers they very often use lenses of poor quality and fail to understand why they cannot produce quality prints. It is also worthwhile buying an enlarger with a filter drawer thus enabling you to do colour work.

Developing a negative
It is a fairly simple job to develop a black and white film, for once a developing tank has been loaded in the darkroom the processing can then be done in daylight. But before you process your first film it is important to practise loading a film on to the spiral of the developing tank. For this purpose we can use a roll of old unimportant exposed film. First, practise loading in the light and then when you feel confident try it in total darkness. It may take a little time at first to acquire the knack but with practice it should not take too long.

The first step in processing a film is to prepare the chemicals – developer, fixer, stopbath – up to the required temperatures. Then *in complete darkness* (first making sure that your hands are thoroughly dry) remove the film from its roll or cassette and load it on to the spiral of the developing tank; place the loaded spiral in the tank and replace the lid on the tank making sure it is securely fitted.

Processing can then be done in daylight as follows:
First, check and make sure that the processing chemicals are at the correct temperature. This can be done by immersing the cylinders containing the chemicals in either hot or cold water baths in order to raise or lower the temperature to the required level. Always wipe the thermometer with the cloth after testing one cylinder of chemical to avoid carrying over drops and contaminating another cylinder.

Next pour the developer into the tank through the opening in the lid and give the spiral several quick twists to dislodge the air bubbles, then agitate according to the manufacturer's instructions for the type of developer you are using. Remember that the development time starts as soon as the developer is poured into the tank.

When the development time is up tip out the developer (keeping the lid on) and pour in the stop bath (which should be at the same temperature as the developer) and agitate for 30 seconds or so. Pour out the stop bath and pour in the fixer which once again should be at the same temperature as the developer and stop bath. Agitate for the first 30 to 60 seconds and then every 30 seconds during the stated fixing time. After the film has been in the fixer for at least a minute you can then lift the lid off the tank and inspect the outer frames of the film, but do *not* unwind the film from the spiral because it is almost impossible to rewind a wet film back on to a spiral. When the film has been fixed it is far easier to wash it in the developing tank.

Washing is very important and a

sudden change of temperature from the development temperature of say 68° will cause reticulation or coarse grain. The way to avoid this is *gradually* to bring the temperature down in the tank, to that of the tap water. Do this by constantly changing the water in the tank and lowering the temperature slightly each time. Once you arrive at tap water temperature you will be able to wash the film under the tap. Do this by using a rubber hose and direct the water down into the bottom of the tank. The water will then come back up the side of the tank, washing the whole of the film. Wash for around 30 to 45 minutes. At the end of the wash add a few drops of wetting agent to the tank water. This helps the water to run off the film and avoids staining. After washing remove the film from the spiral and hang it up to dry in a dust-free room attaching a clip to the bottom of the film to prevent it curling up. Some people advocate the use of a squeegee to remove surplus water but in practice this can sometimes scratch the emulsion. Instead it may be safer to use a damp soft brush, ox hair or sable, to blot off surplus water, froth from the wetting agent or specks of dust. Once the film has dried cut it into strips of six (35mm) or strips of four (6 x 6cm) ready for storage. (See general information).

Recommended film-developer combinations
(All at a temperature of 68°F/20°C)
(a) Ilford FP4 and Aculux, rated at 160ASA. Development times are 6½min for 35mm and 8½min for 120 roll film. This combination gives fine grain and very good contrast. Dilution is 1+9.
(b) Ilford Pan F and ID11, rated at 50ASA. Use developer undiluted and develop for 6 min, for both 35mm and 120 sizes. Gives very fine grain and resolution.
(c) Kodak Plus X and D76, Ilford FP4 and ID11, both rated at 125ASA. Development time for both combinations is 6½min using undiluted developer. These are standard combinations giving good

sharpness, grain and contrast. Developer times are the same for both 35mm and 120 roll film.
(d) Kodak Tri-X and D76, rated at 400ASA, The development time for both 35mm and 120 sizes using undiluted developer is 8min. This is another popular combination giving good results especially with the 120 size film.
(e) Ilford FP4 and Acuspecial, rated at 200ASA. The dilution for this is 1+29 for 35mm and 1+19 for 120 size. Development time for both sizes is 14 min. This combination gives very good fine detail and contrast resulting in a noticeable increase in apparent sharpness and is at its best in high contrast conditions. It requires very careful development.

Although this developer can be used with 120 roll film it is particularly suitable for 35mm work, especially when used with good quality cameras and enlarging equipment.

Printing and enlarging
Having developed the negatives the next step is to make prints from them. Before you start to enlarge the negatives, it is very useful to make contact prints enabling you to select the best pictures for enlarging and saving you hours of unnecessary work and wasted materials.

First, set out the chemicals in dishes in the following order:
1) Developer
2) Stop bath
3) Fixer
4) Water

Temperatures are not as critical as when processing films but it is better to keep all the chemicals at around 68°F/20°C.

Contact strips can be made in the following two ways:

a) Contact printing frame.
Place the strips of film into the contact frame. Then by the light of a safelight only, place a sheet of 8in x 10in printing paper (grade 2) into the printer and close.

b) Plate glass.
With only the safelight on, place the negatives, shiny side up, on top of a

piece of 8in x 10in printing paper (grade 2). Then place a sheet of plate glass (the same size as the printing paper) on top of the negatives. Make sure the glass has been thoroughly cleaned beforehand to avoid marking the negative.

Whichever method you chose to use, exposure is the same for both, either by switching the room light on for two or three seconds or by what is perhaps a more accurate method, using the enlarger. Place the unit on the enlarger baseboard and with the lens at full aperture and at least 2ft from the baseboard, expose for two to three seconds. Remove the paper from unit or glass and proceed to develop the contact sheet. To develop a contact sheet you use the same process as that for general printing, a process described in detail later in this section.

Before describing the enlarging process let us look at the main types of negatives from which you will be making prints. In theory if you have exposed and developed your film correctly you should only need to print the negatives on normal paper (grade two). But in practice it is a different matter. Subjects can be flat or contrasting. Exposures may be wrong because of lighting etc. We may over or under develop the film, and so on. With this in mind, illustrated on page 20 are the most common negative types that you would encounter.
a) Soft, flat, negative lacking contrast. This is usually caused by under-exposure and/ or under-development.
b) Harsh contrasty negative. This type of negative is generally caused by over-exposure and/or over-development.
c) Normal negative. There is a good detail in both the dark (highlight) and light (shadow) areas.

Under each negative is a print made on three different grades of paper. (Printing paper can be obtained in various grades from soft through to hard – grades one to three or four). It will be seen that the soft negative (a) prints well on hard paper – grade three. The contrary negative (b) prints well on soft paper – grade one, and the normal negative (c) is correctly printed on normal paper – grade two. As well as keeping the normal grade of paper in stock it is advisable to have some of the other grades to hand.

Having set out the chemicals (the same as for contact printing), place the strip of negatives in the enlarger, shiny side up, and the opposite way round; this is because when the negative is projected onto the baseboard it will appear the other way round. It is very important, before inserting the negatives into the enlarger, to remove dust particles with a small brush.

Switch on the safelight and switch off the room light. Do not switch on the room light again until the print is fixed. Switch on the enlarger, making sure the lens is at full aperture (wide open). Raise the enlarger head until the negative is framed on the masking frame at the required size. Focus the negative, making absolutely sure that the negative is sharply focused. Then inspect the image and decide what grade of paper is required. Once that is decided stop the lens down by two stops (to increase the depth of focus) and switch off the enlarger.

As it is very difficult to make a perfect print first time it is wise to make a test print. Place a sheet of the correct grade of printing paper in the masking frame (remembering to close the packet of unexposed paper). Then expose for two to five seconds, depending on the size of enlargement. Now cover a small section of the print (say a fifth) with a piece of card and expose again for the same amount of time as the first exposure. Repeat this until you have covered the paper completely. By now you should have five test exposures that are multiples of the first exposure, eg two, four, six, eight, ten seconds.

Next slide the exposed test prints into the developer and agitate by rocking the dish. After 1-3min (depending on the type of paper you are using, resin coated papers require around 1-2min in development and conventional bromide papers be-

tween 1½ and 3min) lift out the print with the developer tongs and place it in the stop bath, without getting the tongs in the stop bath, then putting the tongs back on the side of the developing dish. After agitating for 20sec or so remove the print from the stop bath with the stop bath tongs (not the ones used with the developer) and place in the fixer again without getting the stop bath tongs in the fixer. Agitate for 30sec or so and then turn on the room light.

Inspect the test print, from which we should now be able to judge the correct exposure time for that particular negative.

Next check to make sure the negative is still in focus (having turned off the room light). Now you are ready to make the final print which is processed in exactly the same way as the test print, but giving the correct exposure time. It is important to develop the print fully and never snatch it out of the developer too early. After the print has been fixed for the required time, using the fixer tongs place it in the dish of water in readiness for washing later on. When using tongs do not put the tongs of one dish into the chemical of the next part of the process, otherwise drops of chemical will be transferred back. If you are using resin coated paper washing only takes around five minutes. Just place the dish of prints under a running tap of tepid water if possible and separate them continuously for five minutes. After washing remove surplus water with photographic blotting paper and leave to dry, or alternatively dry with a hair dryer.

Conventional bromide paper prints take between 30 and 45min to wash. They can either be washed in a special print washer or by changing the water in the dish every 5min and at the same time separating the prints once or twice. Repeat this process for up to 45min by which time the prints should be thoroughly washed. After washing remove surplus water with photographic blotting paper and leave to dry, or dry them on a flat bed dryer.

Summarising the printing process:
1 Prepare chemicals to around 20°C.
2 Clean negative and insert into enlarger.
3 Switch on safe light and switch off room lights.
4 Switch on enlarger and raise head to enlarge negative to required size. Focus negative.
5 Inspect negative to decide on grade of printing paper to be used.
6 Stop down lens by two stops and switch off enlarger.
7 Remove printing paper from packet (sealing packet afterwards) and place in masking frame, emulsion side up.
8 Make exposures for test strip.
9 Develop for 1-3min.
10 Stop bath.
11 Fixer.
12 Switch on room light and examine print to determine correct exposure and make sure that the grade of paper is correct.
13 Switch off room light and make final print.
14 Wash prints and dry.
Never allow daylight or room light to fall on unexposed printing paper or it will become fogged.

Glazing
One of the advantages of using resin coated gloss paper is that when the print has been dried it has a very high glaze, but with conventional bromide gloss paper it is necessary to glaze the print to achieve the same high gloss.

To glaze prints we need a chrome glazing sheet large enough to take two or more prints, a rubber roller and if possible a flat bed dryer. The glazing process is as follows:
1 Turn on dryer to recommended setting for glaze.
2 Clean the glazing sheet with a clean damp cloth and then polish with a dry soft cloth.
3 Place the wet prints face down on the glazing sheet and use the rubber roller, working from the centre outwards, to push out the excess water from under the prints. Use blotting paper to mop up the excess water.

Soft flat negative.

Grade three paper (hard).

Harsh contrasty negative.

Grade one paper (soft).

Normal negative.

Grade two paper (normal).

Normal paper.

Soft paper.

Normal paper.

Hard paper.

Soft paper.

Hard paper.

Above is a typical 35mm contact sheet printed on a piece of 10in x 8in printing paper. (Both the 15 exposures of the 645 format and 12 exposures of the 6 x 6cm format fit exactly on a 10in x 8in sheet but for the 10 exposures of the 6 x 7cm size it is necessary to use a 10in x 12in sheet of printing paper.)

Opposite is a test print of picture 17 on the contact sheet (third from left on third line) and below that the final print. It will be seen that the exposure for the final print is around 3 seconds for the foreground and train (allowing for detail in the shadow area) and around 5 seconds for the background and sky. On bigger enlargements the exposures for the test print would obviously be longer, for example 4, 8, 12, 16, 20 seconds etc. Picture details: A4 Pacific 4498 pulls out of Grange-over-Sands with the southbound Cumbrian Coast Express, 22 August 1978.

Camera, Nikkormat with 135mm lens fitted with yellow filter. Exposure 1/250th sec at f4. Film, Ilford Pan F, (rated 50ASA), developed in I D11 undiluted.

22

10   8   6   4   2

4 Place the glazing sheet (with the prints on top) on the dryer, which by now should be at the correct temperature. Bring down, over the prints, the canvas top of the dryer and secure.

5 Leave for 10-15min and then remove canvas top of the dryer by which time the prints should be glazed and will pop off the glazing sheet. If they do not, in no circumstances must you force them off as this will cause blemishes on the glaze. Instead close the canvas top of the glazer again and leave the prints for a few more minutes. If they do not pop off this time it may be because the dryer is not warm enough. If this is the case swab the prints with hot water to remove from the glazing sheet and start the glazing process again when the dryer has heated up.

It is not necessary to use a dryer to glaze your prints. Once the prints have been mounted on the glazing sheet and the excess water removed simply leave them to dry and after an hour or so they should pop off the glazing sheet fully glazed. Obviously by using this method it takes a great deal longer to glaze a batch of prints.

Spotting

It is very difficult to produce a print that is entirely free from blemishes in conditions outside a laboratory. To help the amateur, here is a list of the marks you will frequently meet, with some suggestions on how to correct them. All restoration work is easier on the print than on the negative because of the size, and it is better not to tamper with the original.

The equipment needed is as follows:

A very fine brush, preferably size 00 sable hair; a white saucer and water, and a clean rag; good even lighting; either a stain such as 'Spotone' which penetrates to the paper, or an ink which lies on the surface of the paper; a white pigment such as 'Process White'; also useful are a sharp blade for 'knifing' or a bleach such as 'Spotoff', and

finally – patience.

The usual blemish is the white spot or white hair, caused by dust lying on the surface of the paper during exposure, or lying on the negative. Dust often sticks to the negative when it is hanging up to dry, so a draught-free room is useful in avoiding this. Static also attracts dust to these surfaces, so try not to wear synthetic clothing that crackles in the dark.

White marks are easier to hide in a textured background such as trees, and difficult in pale featureless skies. If using a stain, dilute to a paler shade and stipple a very small amount with the tip of the brush, which should be damp, not dripping. Let this dry first as it will darken, and apply more if needed. If using an ink, remember that this lies on the surface, and as it dries it tends to leave a 'halo' of darker ink. Anticipate this by using a lighter tone, first diluting the ink in a saucer; when it is dry, touch up the paler centre of the halo with a little more ink. Resin coated papers are tricky as the ink tends to blob; a binder such as a little pigment mixed with the ink is helpful. Scratches from wiping the water off the negative are usually white and very fine; they need more practice to correct.

Another blemish is the black mark from a tear in the negative. If it is small, it is easy to nick it out of the paper with a sharp blade, and reglaze the spot with a little gum arabic such as 'Gloy'. If it is a large mark, it is better to bleach it out, and stipple in the white area with stains until the patch blends with the background. This technique can be used to obliterate the odd gricer – the unthinking enthusiast – who rushes up at the last minute, right in your shot.

Other blemishes are not so simple, and need covering with a white or blended pigment. Iron marks, those small brown craters in the surface, are found in some parts of the country, arising from the water supply. Another mark is the grey bruise from rough handling with tongs in the developing bath. The remedy is prevention. A darker

The upper picture of rebuilt West Country Pacific No 34036 *Westward Ho* at speed near Basing with a down Bournemouth train on 8 April 1966 is now history but is completely spoilt by the telegraph pole sticking out of the boiler; other blemishes are a black spot in the exhaust and several white spots in the sky above.

The lower picture shows the restoration work complete with the pole bleached out with 'Spotoff'. This compound comes in two parts, mixed in proportion according to the control of speed required. After the print has been completely washed apply the compound to the wet print until the bleaching out is complete. Then the print is washed briefly and re-fixed for around a minute. Wash the print again and dry and then retouch the white area remaining with dilute stains to match the surrounds. If using glossy paper *do not* glaze the print until this final bleaching is complete.

This process is useful for salvaging historic photographs and modern scenes when for example someone stands in the shot at the last minute. However prevention at the time the picture is taken is always better than cure!

Camera, Konica range-finder, 45mm fixed lens with yellow filter. Exposure 1/500th sec at f5·6. Film, Kodak Plus X, developed in D76 (undiluted).

grey ring in the middle of your print is perhaps the most difficult to cover-up, and is caused by the filament of the bulb in your enlarger. Check that you have the right bulb, and that all the pieces of your enlarger are in place. Ordinary light bulbs are unsuitable because of the bulb details printed across the glass.

Mounting and presentation

For home use (as described in the general information section) you may wish to keep your prints in albums but for exhibition work you will need a more formal presentation, mounting individual photographs on card mounts like pictures. The white edge left by some masking frames should always be trimmed off squarely, using either a blade and ruler or a rotary trimmer.

The card should be thick, matt surfaced, and of a colour that will not detract from the photograph. Some people prefer white, some black and others prefer a neutral tone such as elephant or donkey. Black and white prints are better on a shade with little colour, while colour prints can stand a hue such as puce, evergreen or slate.

The size and placing are also matters of choice. If the print is small and historic, it would benefit from a large mount. If the print is very large, the mount could be trimmed to match the edges – 'block mounting'. Some people prefer an even width of border, others mount the print slightly higher than centre. However, if you are displaying a set of prints you must be consistent.

These are two ways of fixing the photograph on the card, either by glue or by adhesive sheets. Glues come in liquid form or in aerosol sprays or adhesive sticks. Some rely on the solvent drying out, some need heat to melt the contacts.

The important things to watch for are that the glue does not spread in ridges, that the solvent has time to evaporate before pressing the print down – very important with resin coated papers, that you can have a second chance to position the prints,

and that you can remove any blobs of glue at the edges. It is always best to mark in at least one edge with a fine pencil line on the card to guide your placement, making sure that it is square with the edges.

Aerosols such as Scotch Photo Mount have adjustable spray widths for economy, allow for repositioning and become permanent after 10min. Cover your work table with rough paper and spray both surfaces to be glued, using a mask of scrap paper over the card that will show. Position the print and rub down with a soft cloth working from the centre outwards to avoid trapping air bubbles. Stick adhesives such as Pritt look like a giant lip salve. Wipe the stick over both surfaces, masking the card etc. This method is handy for small prints.

Spread-on glues such as Cow Gum need a very thin coating on both surfaces, using a wide-edged spreader to avoid ridges. Protect your table with rough paper, apply the adhesive thinly and give it a few minutes for the solvent fumes to evaporate. Position and rub down from the centre. Any smears of glue can be rubbed off with a clean rag.

Rubber solution glues such as Copydex are used in much the same way, being careful when spreading not to touch any dry glue which will pull in rubbery threads. Positioning has to be right first time for this reason.

Patersons produce a Thermal Print Mountant in liquid form, which you apply with a brush to both surfaces and leave to dry for half an hour. When you have positioned your print cover it with a clean sheet of paper and iron it down with a cool to medium heat setting. This is safe with resin coated papers. Dry Mounting Tissue also uses heat to stick the print down. The sheet of tissue should not project beyond the edge of the photograph. The easiest way to make sure of this is to start with an untrimmed print. Lay your tissue on the back of the photograph and hold it in place with a few dabs with the tip of a hot iron, then trim both together. If your print is already

trimmed, tack down the tissue with the iron and trim away the surplus with a blade. Position the print on the card, protect with paper and iron with a medium hot iron – it is best to experiment on scraps, particularly with resin coated papers. If the tissue does not quite stick to the card, apply more heat; if the tissue sticks to the card, but the print comes away, iron again using a lower setting.

The finished mount looks good when left perfectly plain, but some like to frame the photo with a single line, about a centimetre from the edges. If using ink, you can use a fountain pen or ruling pen with a width adjustment. Draw a pencil line as a guide, and turn your ruler over, to prevent ink from creeping under the edge. It is better to use less ink and go over the line again. Always test on a spare piece of card before you work on the actual mount.

If you are exhibiting, write your name, title and description of the photograph on the back, for the benefit of those compiling the catalogue. If you want the title to appear on the front, you can draw directly onto the card freehand or by a stencil, or you can apply transfer letters for a professional finish.

Shading and dodging

Shading and dodging simply means giving different exposures to different areas of the negative. This is very relevant to railway photography for it would be fair to say that the great majority of railway photographs need a certain amount of shading and dodging, some to a far greater degree than others.

There are two main reasons for this. The first is the need to show good details in the sky, an important feature when photographing any kind of traction, but especially important when photographing steam as a heavy exhaust (which is invariably set against the sky) from a steam engine and sometimes from a diesel. It can turn an ordinary picture into something very exciting, conveying the power and the strength of the locomotive. To some extent the sky and exhaust can be brought out more on the negative by the use of filters (see previous chapter). Nevertheless even when using a filter the sky and exhaust usually require more exposure at the printing stage than the main body of the negative.

The second important point (often forgotten) is the foreground. In railway photographs the foreground frequently consists of station platforms, track ballast, grass verges and banks. As we usually expose for the main scene – the train – the foreground, like the sky and exhaust, tend to be a little over exposed and need extra exposure at the printing stage. It is very important to have good strong foreground tones, perhaps a little on the dark side to focus attention on the main subject.

There are two methods of shading, either by using your hands, a technique used by professional printers or by using a dodging and shading kit which can either be bought at photographic stores or made at home.

Using your hands to shade can be tricky and you may find it easier to use a set of home-made shaders and dodgers. This consists of two pieces of 10in x 8in card (which covers all prints up to 10in x 8in size) one of them being plain and the other having a hole cut into the card roughly off centre. The hole is about one inch across. The other dodger consists of a small round piece of card about ¾in across, attached to a piece of wire, 8in in length. You will find that these usually cover any contingency.

Most railway pictures will require extra exposure in the sky and foreground and this can be achieved by burning in these parts. After developing the test print check the sky and foreground and you will usually find that to get an equal balance of tones all over the picture more exposure will need to be given to either one or both of these than to the main body of the picture. This is where the first of our home-made shaders comes in – the 10in x 8in piece of plain card. After exposing

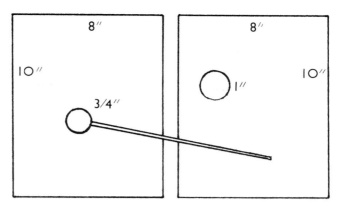

Fig 4 Shaders and dodgers.

the print for the correct time for the main picture switch off the enlarger. Then hold the 10in x 8in card about three to four inches above the paper (to increase the shadow area) covering everything except the sky. Switch on enlarger and expose for the correct time for the sky but at the same time keep the card moving slightly to prevent a line appearing on the finished print where you have shaded in. Switch off the enlarger but if needed repeat the process, but this time give extra exposure to the foreground. Then process the print in normal way. Be very careful when shading to avoid knocking the enlarger which would cause vibrations and ruin the print.

The technique of using the other dodgers is similar to the last. The 10in x 8in card with a small hole in it is used to burn in small things like buffer beams, locomotive numbers, reporting numbers and the like. If the section to be burned-in is on the edges of the picture raise the card towards the enlarger head which increases the shadow size, thus enabling you to move the card off centre and still cover the main part of the picture. The small circular card on wire is used to hold back smaller details, especially front ends of locomotives (when the photograph is taken against back lighting), wheels and any other smaller items that need less exposure than the main picture.

At first you will find it difficult to shade and dodge prints but in time with perseverance most people

achieve a fair degree of success. It is worthwhile keeping your early efforts at shading and after a period of time make a comparison with your current work. You should be very pleasantly surprised.

Double Printing

Double printing requires much care and attention to achieve reasonable results, but can be very useful in railway photography.

For example you may have a good sharp negative of a rare steam locomotive at work but because the photograph was taken on a very warm summer's day no exhaust is showing. By double printing we can add an exhaust from another negative and bring the original picture to life.

A word of caution – this technique is usually only successful when the locomotive is set against the sky, since it is more or less impossible to double print against a background of anything else.

The technique for double printing is:

1 Take a piece of card the same size as the print required and place in the masking frame on the enlarger baseboard.

2 Place negative of train in enlarger and expose on to card and then having focused etc draw the outline of train and horizon on card. Switch off enlarger.

3 Remove card from masking frame and by cutting round outline of train and horizon divide card into two masks, marking them "top" and "bottom".

4 Place printing paper into masking frame and swing red filter into position (to cover lens) then turn on enlarger.

5 Place the top mask round the top of the train and horizon so that the sky is covered. Uncover the lens by moving the red filter and make an exposure. Then switch off the enlarger.

6 Once again swing red filter into position, turn on enlarger. Remove top mask and replace with bottom mask which covers the train and landscape. Switch off enlarger.

7 Remove negative of train and replace with negative of exhaust to be printed in.

8 Swing red filter into position and turn on enlarger.

9 Line up exhaust with chimney of locomotive making sure that the exhaust is in focus.

10 Uncover the lens by moving the red filter and make an exposure. Process print as normal.

It is very important to place the masks correctly or you will finish up with an obvious join.

Double printing is a very skilful process and so expect quite a few failures before success is achieved.

Composing on the enlarger baseboard.

Developing and printing the negative has almost as much magic about it as being out on the lineside. To-day, even after many years of railway photography, I never cease to be thrilled at being able to capture on film that split second of action. And after a day filming I am always eager to develop the film usually the same night if possible or at the very latest by the next day and then print the negative as soon as possible after that.

When you are out photographing you compose your pictures in the viewfinder and after developing the film you generally print the negative more or less as it is. But there are quite a few occasions when you can do some composition work, often quite radical, on the enlarger baseboard.

Once you have the negative in the enlarger, focused and ready to print, look carefully at the composition because it may be that by some

These two pictures well illustrate baseboard composition. The picture on the left is a print of the whole of the negative which as it stands is obviously not very satisfactory from a composition point of view. By drastic cropping we finish up with the picture on the right which gives us a much more satisfactory composition because the centre of interest (front end of the train) falls on the Golden section and also has curved lines (rails and exhaust) leading to that point.

Another frame was shot after this one in which the train was balanced up with the signalbox on the left, which meant I was able to obtain two satisfactory pictures.

It will be noted that the finished print is only 2/5ths of the original negative which ably demonstrates the quality of today's better 35mm lenses and cameras especially when used with fine grain film like Ilford Pan F.

Picture details: Class 9F 2–10–0 *Evening Star* at speed near Micklefield with the morning York Circular train, 9 July 1978.

Camera, Nikkormat with 50mm standard lens plus yellow filter. Exposure 1/500th sec at f4. Film, Ilford Pan F (50ASA), developed in I D11 (undiluted).

fairly simple adjustments you can alter this with startling results.

One very simple thing that you can do is to change the format of the picture from horizontal to vertical and vice versa. To do this you may need to enlarge or decrease the picture size accordingly. Many photographs have started out life as horizontals and finished up as vertical compositions. Never be afraid to crop your pictures. When you inspect the pictures on the baseboard keep a large piece of card handy and use it to cover different portions of the picture. Your picture may look flat at 10in x 8in but may come alive cropped down to say 10in x 5in. Look at the many fine pictures in books and magazines that are not of conventional sizes.

Be prepared to experiment with your compositions and you will find that this adds another enjoyable and satisfying dimension to dark-room work.

Print quality

Once you have mastered the technique for developing a monochrome print and are able to produce a reasonable photograph it is very important to concentrate on producing a first class print.

A top quality print is one that contains a good range of tones from black through to white, with plenty of detail in the shadow areas and above all one that is sharp all over. For this you obviously require a good sharp negative with an average amount of contrast and good detail throughout. You can achieve reasonable prints from negatives that lack some of these requirements (with the obvious exception of sharpness) but generally to achieve a top quality print you need a first class negative.

Provided that they are careful and consistent during processing, most photographers, after a certain period of trial and error, will begin

to produce good negatives. There will always be the negative that because of lighting conditions or mis-calculation is not quite up to standard but if you take care they should not be too numerous.

Thus assuming that we have developed a roll of film to the required standard and made a contact sheet, before we start to enlarge and print the negatives we must do two very important things:
(a) Inspect the contact sheet and pick out the best compositions.
(b) Look at the corresponding negatives and place them in order of difficulty beginning with the one that you think will be the easiest to print and finishing with the hardest.

At first you may find this difficult to do but you can take it as a general guide that a negative with a good tonal range, fairly even lighting and a small amount of shadow area is usually easier to print than one taken with back lighting and therefore with plenty of shadows and contrast, if only because as a rule less shading and dodging is required with the first type of negative. Always start with the easiest negative because once you have a couple of prints processed to your satisfaction it is then easier psychologically to tackle the more difficult ones.

Having selected your negative and placed it in the enlarger (remembering to remove any dust and hair), once you have it to the required size on the baseboard take great care over the focusing, checking that it is pin-sharp all over. Sometimes the enlarger head may be slightly out of alignment causing one edge to be out of focus. The foam on the bottom of the masking frame may be worn at one side and this may cause focusing problems. It is important to check on all these things to ensure picture sharpness. Using a glassless negative carrier in the enlarger can also be a cause of

unsharpness because of the popping of negatives as they warm up; this is particularly so when using the larger negative sizes. Always check the focus before every exposure (remembering to stop the lens down again once this has been done).

Always make a test print; this will save you time and materials as well as being a vital factor in the achievement of a first rate print.

Never under develop your print. Always allow full development time and a little extra if necessary. This is essential to obtain a full range of tones. Experience will tell you when a print is ready to be removed from the developer. A point worth noting is that a print will darken slightly when it is dried, so that if it appears a little on the light side when being washed it may be alright once it has been dried.

It is always very important to wash prints for at least the required time. This will ensure permanence. If your prints have not been washed sufficiently, after a period of – possibly months or years – stains will begin to appear and ruin the print. This also applies if they have not been fixed for the correct amount of time in which case the prints will begin to turn brown, once again ruining them and of course wasting hours of work and materials. It is also essential that you should be as clean and tidy in your darkroom as is possible, ensuring that the enlarging equipment is regularly dusted and cleaned, particularly before use, and that all processing equipment is thoroughly washed before and after use.

All these factors should help towards high quality printing but in addition it is important to study other photographers' work especially at exhibitions etc. It is here that you should be able to see what a top class print really looks like and make comparisons with your own work.

3
Colour Photography

The most satisfying composition in colour will have the same 'skeleton' as a black and white picture, for it will rely on a structure that has lines or connections directing your eyes to the focus of interest. It will have balance of detail and balance in the placing of light and dark, but with the added ingredient of placing a strong colour against a subdued colour. It will also have interesting patterns or surface details. Without these, your picture will be just an ordinary snapshot and never make the front cover of your magazine. Speaking of magazines, we owe a lot to the colour supplements of several Sunday newspapers, which have done so much to open our eyes to colour and pattern in unexpected places. The newspaper photographers are really artists who have taught us by their skill in composition to see the world in a fresh light. Many of their pictures still hold our attention by their underlying quality, long after their news value has faded.

It is more difficult to take a good railway colour picture on several counts, the first being that the element of colour stacks up the odds against keeping out distracting features. It is much easier with black and white prints to spot out the last-minute gricer who rushes into your shot, by turning him into a tree! It is difficult in colour to disguise the family dressed in fluorescent anoraks who will move into the middle of the open field in your line of sight just as you are about to take an approaching steam special. Other things can get in the way, such as cars. There is no need to park right by a level crossing, when you could pull-up on a verge ten yards back, leaving the view clear. Perhaps you do want something

bright in the foreground, but dozens of other photographers might not like your choice of colour.

The colours of the rainbow, or spectrum, range from visible indigo blue, (ultra violet being invisible) through greens and yellows to deepest red. White daylight is a mixture of all these, and objects reflect the parts of the spectrum which are appropriate, ie they have colours. Objects lit by only one colour, such as by signal lights or by sodium street lamps, can only appear in the colour available. In nature the blue colours we perceive tend to appear on the horizon and in the sky; in other words they are faraway. Blue colours tend to fill in wide areas and form backgrounds. Blue is the colour seen best by the retina of the eye when the light is dim, as at night, and when the pupil of the eye is on wide aperture. Therefore by association, blue is a receding colour, restful and non-aggressive. Red, on the other hand, is a dominant penetrating colour, and is used to alert us to danger. Conveniently, the wavelengths of red light travel better over long distances than green or blue, which is why red is used to signal 'stop' to a train far away, and why green can be used when the locomotive is waiting for 'go' by the gantry. Reds and yellows are also sunny colours and, by association, photographs using these colours tend to have a happy feeling, whereas pictures showing much blue tend to be wistful or melancholy like a rainy day. The exception would depend on the brightness and intensity of the blue, such as an engine painted in Caledonian Blue, standing in brilliant sunshine. It was one of the French Impressionists who said that 'one square metre of blue is

bluer than one square centimetre.'

If you want your picture to have depth, make sure that the background is misty and has a blue or green cast, and that your subject, ie the locomotive, shows the red buffer beam, in the case of steam, or the yellow front of the cab, in the case of a diesel. When an engine is travelling at speed towards you and want to convey this impression, this dramatic device of the bright red or yellow in the foreground never fails. The train jumps out of the picture. Indeed on some transparencies the red is almost three-dimensional against a blue-green background. There are other things which you can use in the foreground to establish nearness. Signals are a good example, especially the red/white sides of semaphore arms, or the yellow fishtails of distant signals. Level crossing gates are another, and posts bearing numbers painted yellow. Some photographers place bunches of flowers in strategic places to liven-up the scene, but probably conservationists would object most strongly. A gorse bush in full bloom would be much better, or in winter, a patch of bracken.

The red/green contrast demonstrates in colour the same principle of contrast in black and white. It is a colour version of tonal recession, whereby objects of strongly contrasted light and dark stand out, and misty grey areas recede. This is a similar effect to that of focusing on a close object leaving the background a blur. Any strong contrast will stand out, for example the white lamps on the front of a black smokebox, or the black and yellow stripes on a diesel shunter. If the locomotive is rather dirty and drab, you must try to find some contrast.

Colour 1.
Dent station on the Settle and Carlisle route, 22 May 1982. Southern Railway 4–6–0 No 777 *Sir Lamiel* charges through the station with a SLOA southbound Cumbrian Mountain Express.

Camera, Nikon FM with series E36–72mm zoom lens set at 50mm, plus ultra-violet filter. Film, Kodachrome 64ASA. Exposure 1/250th sec at f4.

This picture demonstrates the basic structure of composition found in monochrome photographs. The strong shapes of the bridge arches echo the curves of the boiler front and smoke deflectors, and these contrast with the two white squares and the two triangular trees. All the lines lead the eye to the chimney on the Golden Section. The red buffer beam shows how the dominant colour jumps out of the page.

The head-on viewpoint minimising any sideways movement was chosen as Dent is frequently cloudy and dark, which would have needed a wider aperture and/or a slower shutter speed. Fortunately the sun shone, if but weakly, and gave that extra sparkle to a delightful scene.

Colour 2.
Jubilee class 4–6–0 No 5690 *Leander* climbs through Chinley on 24 February 1979 with a Guide Bridge–York special.

Camera, Nikon FM with 50mm lens and ultra-violet filter. Film, Kodachrome 64ASA. Exposure 1/250th sec at f5·6.

This illustrates the use of dynamic diagonals and a triangular structure composition. This location makes use of the last of the winter snow to reflect more light on to the sides of the locomotive in an otherwise dark cutting. The snow also enhances the visual impact of the white steam and the white panels of the carriage.

Colour 3.
26 August 1981. LNER Pacific No 4498 *Sir Nigel Gresley* emerges from Culgaith tunnel (north of Appleby) with the southbound Cumbrian Mountain Express.

Camera, Nikon FM with 50mm lens plus ultra-violet filter. Film,

Kodachrome 64ASA. Exposure 1/500th sec at f4·5.

This composition in the primary colours blue and yellow, and their secondary green, shows how the recessive blue can be dominant if it is bright enough. The Garter blue of Sir Nigel Gresley *is given an extra boost here by the intense colour of the cloudless sky, and the contrasting yellow of the dry grass in the cutting. On a monochrome level, the strongest contrasts are found in the white steam and black smoke, and in the silhouette of the black front against the sunny bank, all in the focus-of-interest area. Notice too how the eye is carried to the front of the engine by the slopes of the bank and the shape of the trees on the skyline.*

Colour 4.
An Inter-City 125 bound for Bristol hurries through the Birmingham outskirts near the University on 9 June 1982.

Camera, Nikon FM with series E36 – 72mm zoom lens set at 45mm plus ultra-violet filter. Film, Kodachrome 64ASA. Exposure 1/500th sec at f3·5.

Yellow and red are generally considered to be dominant, sunny colours. Here the glow of a summer's evening is captured in the warm yellow of the cab and the soft red of the bridge behind. This scene is completed by the rich deep greens of the surrounding trees.

HSTs are painted with strong horizontal lines, which can present a problem to the photographer. Here the lines are broken up by the patches of shadow from the overhanging trees, while the area of heavy shade in the foreground is relieved by the stalks of cow parsley.

Colour 5.
LMS Pacific No 46229 *Duchess of Hamilton* storms into Wennington on a photographic run past on 12 April 1982. The train is a Carnforth–Leeds special organised by SLOA. Run pasts are a feature of SLOA trains and this photograph illustrates what can be achieved by passengers.

Camera, Nikon FM with 50mm lens plus ultra-violet filter. Film, Kodachrome 64ASA. Exposure 1/500th sec at f5·6.

This powerful composition in red and grey leaves no doubt in the viewer's eye about the focus-of-interest. The velvet texture of the exhaust is repeated in the trees still in their winter grey, and the darkness of its shadow is balanced with touches of white steam from the valves, the lamps and the gate behind the wall. A little green in the field helps to make the red even stronger.

Colour 6.
On the evening of 24 October 1981 4–6–0 No 850 *Lord Nelson* rests at York station after arriving with a special train from Carlisle.

Camera, Nikon FM with 35mm lens plus ultra-violet filter. Film, Kodachrome 64ASA. Exposure 1 min, 15 sec at f4.

This night study was taken with available light from the platform lamps and the signals, while the near side of the locomotive and coaches was lit by the flash guns of photographers just off the left-hand edge of the picture. The daylight film shows the flashlight as a blue-white colour, while the tungsten lamps show as a warm yellow. The weather that night was unpleasant, with blustery wind and rain, as seen in the exhaust. The camera and tripod were shielded behind a barrier and under a coat. The wet sleepers reflect the lights and bring more interest into an otherwise dark foreground.

Colour 7.
The evening sun glints on South African Railways class 14CR 4–8–2 No 1897 as it shunts at Riversdale on the Worcester–George line.

Camera, Nikkormat with 50mm lens plus ultra-violet filter. Film, Kodachrome 64ASA. Exposure 1/250th sec at f4.

This picture shows another way of making the most of the available light. The setting sun reflects off the rails at one point, so that the photographer knows exactly where the engine will glitter most brightly. Whatever the colour of the locomotive, it will show as orange, the colour of the sun. With this type of 'glint' shot great care must be taken to shield the camera lens from the rays of the sun, otherwise the picture will be spoilt by excessive flare.

1▲   2▼

3▲

4▼

▲ 5

6▲

7▼

9▲

10▼

11▲

12▲

13

14▼

Colour 8.

A Turkish Railways 2–8–2 (built by Robert Stephenson & Co) with an evening local train from Izmir to Ciyli, 25 February 1976.

Camera, Agfa Super Isolette, folding 6 x 6 camera with 75mm lens. Film, Agfa CT18 (120 size), 50ASA. Exposure 1/125th sec at f5·6.

When the light has almost gone, one way to take a moving train is to treat it as a silhouette. In these conditions, the photographer must find an interesting background; cloud formations coloured by the setting sun are one possibility, water is another, especially with ripples reflecting the light from the sky. This nocturne was taken with the engine going away, so that the camera picked up the glow of the fire – the perfect finishing touch.

Colour 9.

Povoa shed, northern Portugal, on the evening of 24 September 1974. Being serviced is E142, one of four narrow gauge 2–8–2T engines built by Henschel in 1931.

Camera, Nikkormat with 50mm lens plus ultra-violet filter. Film, Agfa CT18 50ASA. Exposure 1/125th sec at f5·6.

When the engine and its surroundings are black, there is not much point in taking a colour picture unless the photographer can find something colourful to relieve the gloom. This picture shows two possibilities, the background and the workers. The buildings at the back with their red roofs and immaculate white walls, throw the black engine into strong relief, while the workmen are wearing blue and orange shirts, forming a secondary focus of interest.

Colour 10.

British Rail Class 45 diesel No 45104 enters Loughborough with a St Pancras–Nottingham train, 12 June 1982.

Camera, Nikon FM with series E36 – 72 zoom lens set at approximately 45mm plus ultra-violet filter. Film, Kodachrome 64ASA. Exposure 1/250th sec at f4.

The middle of the day often presents problems with lighting the subject, especially when the sun is in line with the rails and behind the locomotive as in this case. The highlights and shadows are strongly contrasted, and little detail underneath is visible. However, this picture is saved by using the diffused light under the canopy to

provide the middle tones, while the sunlit edge of the platform reflects some light into the shadows on the engine itself. Incidentally, this is a useful record of station architecture, showing the cast-iron brackets to advantage.

Colour 11.

This picture was taken inside the cab of a South African Railways class 24 2–8–4 locomotive at George on 26 July 1976.

Camera, Nikkormat with 35mm lens plus ultra-violet filter. Film, Kodachrome 64ASA. Exposure 1/60th sec at f2.8.

It would have been almost impossible to have taken this picture without using a medium wide angle lens. As it was I stood right at the back of the cab in order to get a reasonable coverage of this beautiful footplate.

The lighting was even and diffuse, coming from three sides of the cab, which showed the polished copper and brass to good advantage. If the sun had been shining directly on the fittings, the intense highlights and shadows would have lost the colour of the metal. The fire had cooled down to a pleasing red; if it had been roaring at full blast it would have only shown up as a yellow square.

Colour 12.

Sunset at Capital Park shed, Pretoria. The date is 13 August 1982 and the locomotive is a class 15 CA 4–8–2 No 2852.

Camera, Nikon FM with 135mm lens plus ultra-violet filter. Film, Kodachrome 25ASA. Exposure 1/125th sec at f5·6.

This dramatic mood picture relies on the brilliant red of the sunset for its impact. To obtain direct shots of the disc of the sun, it is advisable to wait until the last moment before the sun finally sets, when the haze in the atmosphere filters the light to a usable level, so avoiding the risk of flare. Also, to make the sun appear larger in proportion to the scene, a medium telephoto lens was used.

Colour 13.

This beautiful setting is Victoria Bridge on the Severn Valley Railway and the scene shows LMS mogul No 6443 with a Bridgnorth–Bewdley train, 14 October 1979.

Camera, Nikon FM with 85mm lens plus ultra-violet filter. Film, Kodachrome 64ASA. Exposure 1/500th sec at f5·6.

This peaceful river scene is composed almost entirely of shades of green. Like the previous picture of the sunset, it has strong monochrome construction, with the greatest tonal contrast appearing at the focus-of-interest. Trees play an important part here; the central tree leads the eye to the engine, while the fringe of branches at the left-hand edge help to 'anchor' the free end of the bridge.

Colour 14.

Deltic diesel No 55007 *Pinza* bursts under Holgate Junction bridge and into the evening sunshine as it leaves York with the 19.10 to Kings Cross, 24 May 1981.

Camera, Nikon FM with 50mm lens plus ultra-violet filter. Film, Kodachrome 64ASA. Exposure 1/250th sec at f5·6.

One way to photograph a long thin shape is to accentuate the form by enclosing it in a narrow slot. This massive structure of the bridge and its shadow trap the Deltic like the teeth of a crocodile. This approach is the reverse of the upper picture where the engine is dark against a lighter background; here the train appears bright and colourful contrasted against the black girders.

You might silhouette it against a light shed wall, or a brightly-coloured container wagon, or even against the sky; the orange disc of the setting sun or the clouds around it, make a stunning impact. On shed, you might find a worker in a new boilersuit who would be happy to pose at the chimney end. Even a pile of oil drums could be pressed into service.

Some locomotives blend into the landscape because of the colours they are painted, especially in the distance, such as *Sir Nigel Gresley*, painted Garter Blue, the preserved green Deltic, and Great Western locomotives. Other greens such as *Lord Nelson*, tend to clash with the landscape and must be sited with care. The human eye is very sensitive to greens and can tell the difference between more similar shades than in reds. Fortunately colour films are designed to match what we see though there may be a slight cast in one brand compared with another.

You might want to try using the theme of one colour for your photograph, instead of exploiting contrasts, and create a 'mood' picture. You would have to search out locations that enhanced the colour of your subject. You might find *Sir Nigel Gresley* on the Cumbrian Coast route running by water on a day when the sky and sea were blue. *King George V* looks very handsome on a summer's day running up the Welsh Marches through pastures and broad-leaved trees. The yellow nose of an HST echoes the intense yellow of fields of rape in May. *Princess Elizabeth* or *Duchess of Hamilton* could be photographed passing brick walls of factories. A Western diesel, painted in the putty-coloured livery, could be found a setting by a quarry or landslip. A bright-red locomotive on the Lakeside Railway might pass by a bank of corn poppies, or that lilac colliery engine at Carnforth could one day stand by waste ground covered in purple fireweed. Even someone's washing on a clothes line might tone in with your engine. You will find many more applica-

tions of this idea of the colour theme once you start looking.

Different brands of film have slightly different colour casts. You will have to experiment to find the one you like and stick to it, especially if you intend to give slide shows, because if your magazine contains a random jumble of greenish slides or reddish slides, the effect will be disturbing. Some makes of lens are noted for their colour contrast, others give a softer blend of colours. Your final choice of film may depend on which one suits your lens resolution, and here your photographic supplier should be able to advise you. The use of filters will also be a determining factor in the colour cast of your pictures. These are described in the section on filters. When buying film for outdoor daylight use and (blue) flash photography, make sure that you get the right sort, not the film for indoor work by tungsten lamps. Indoor film will give you photographs of the outside world with a pronounced blue cast, while outdoor film used by artificial light will give you an orange cast. There are compensating filters for those interested in experimenting with these effects.

Colour films, in addition to being balanced for certain lighting conditions, are made in different speeds, marked in ASA or in DIN ratings (see glossary). The most widely used speeds are 64ASA for slide transparencies and 100ASA for colour negative film. Many other speeds are available; 25ASA is excellent in very sunny countries and gives brilliant detail; much faster speeds for specialist applications can be obtained, but generally the faster the film, the coarser the grain.

The next problem to consider is the quantity of light. There is usually not enough. Your train has been delayed and missed its path, it is getting dark and you are cold, and stuck with 64ASA film. So you have the following choices: you could try to "freeze" the movement of the locomotive, even on 1/125thsec, by taking it almost head-on, when the

train makes very little movement across the line of vision; you could treat it as a silhouette and forget the shadow detail – this is particularly good for dawn or sunset shots on bridges; you could treat it as a 'nocturne', making sure that there are plenty of lights in cottage windows, etc; you could take the picture at a great distance, reducing the visible movement; you could set your camera on a much longer exposure and take the moving streak of light; or you could try a panned shot. It helps to have a tripod and cable release, in these circumstances, to ensure freedom from camera shake if you are shivering. If you want to attempt the standard 'three-quarter front' shot, you will be using the widest aperture possible in order to keep the shutter speed fast. This means that the depth of field that will be in focus will be shallow. It is better to set your focus on one predetermined spot and take the best shot you can, than attempt two or three, and try to cope with winding-on and focusing at the same time, when the train is hurtling down on you at 60mph.

There are times when subdued daylight is an advantage, such as when you are photographing very shiny surfaces, or trying to show the brilliant colour of the paintwork. If the sun is very bright then the colours will be lost in the intense light and shade. A light haze over the sun is very good in these circumstances, or reflected light. This can be found shining back from station walls and platforms, or from light-coloured goods wagons. The principle is the same as using a white umbrella in portrait photography. You can also create some exciting effects by looking at engines reflected in very shiny paintwork or brightly polished brass fittings, or including the colour of something just out of sight of the camera by lending its colour to the scene in the reflections. You could experiment with this idea at your leisure in a railway museum.

Exposure in these conditions depends on what you want to emphasise, either the sparkle of shiny surfaces or the colour of the groundwork. To be on the safe side you could 'bracket the exposure' by taking shots over and under the exposure that you think appropriate. Beware of the reflected image of the sun burning straight into your lens and upsetting your reading. Try to interpose some relevant object, or move slightly so that the image comes into a dull or non-reflecting area.

Reflected sunlight has its uses. When the train is late and the sun is setting, you will find that the rails shine brightly at one particular point, the 'flash point'. Aim to take your picture there, as the sun will be reflected off the locomotive like a lighthouse beam. And that glorious sight will make up for all the trials and tribulations of the day.

Most railway photographers send away their colour films to be processed. If you do, your compositions will come back exactly as you took them. If you are using colour negative film it is an easy matter to have selective enlargements made. This is also the case if you intend to make prints from slides. (The Cibachrome process of making prints from slides is described later in this chapter.)

However, with slides that are intended primarily for projection, generally you are stuck with the picture that you took, so here are a few guides to making better pictures (which of course apply to all types of film.) First, remember that the camera takes in a little more at the edges than you see through the viewfinder, particularly if you wear glasses which prevents you from getting your eye close to the viewfinder. Scan the surroundings beforehand for any unwanted features, and leave a generous margin as safety. It is a good idea to negotiate with fellow enthusiasts about their final disposition of elbows etc. Pick out guiding marks through your viewfinder and tell yourself not to swing past them. Straps are another hazard; they have a habit of poking into the shot. One way round this is to use limp straps of a conspicuous colour. The

colour will remind you to check, and limp straps tuck into the palm, clear of the trigger finger. If a fluorescent anorak appears on the scene you can stick a few weeds (common, not rare) between you and the offending object, and crouch. Last minute arrivals are a problem, as the bellowed entreaties to get out of the way are picked up by sound-cine-cameras and tape recorders. Nothing must distract from the principal actor on the stage – the train.

It is important to fill the frame. If the view is noted for some feature such as a gas-holder, a castle or a particular hill, then it should form the secondary focal point of interest and complement the locomotive. If the line passes through a pleasant though ordinary landscape, then choose trees and buildings that will frame the centre of interest, and not be cropped off at ridiculous points. If the landscape is flat and featureless, then either the sky must have some interesting clouds or steam exhaust, or the engine must fill the frame itself. Remember to let the locomotive come in towards you just that little bit more, as you have to account for that extra width at the edges.

It is tempting to start taking the train when it is too distant, especially if you are afraid that the locomotive, in the case of steam, will cut off for a slack before it reaches you. Perhaps a short telephoto lens would be better for you. Another solution is to choose a view that has alternatives: raised up to show the steam, or dropped down to let the engine fill the upper part of the frame, while showing something interesting in the lower half or foreground, if the driver should shut off steam.

These points should form a sound basis for obtaining reliably good photographs. Once the photographer has mastered them, he will no doubt want to experiment and produce pictures which catch the eye through their originality.

Making color prints from slides.
Colour work today is not the compli-

cated process that it used to be and it is now relatively easy to make prints from transparencies. This should appeal to the many railway photographers who use colour slide film.

The advantages of transparencies are numerous. We have slides with which to give both private and public slide shows (which are very popular among railway societies) and at the same time by using such processes as Cibachrome we can make prints from transparencies, thus being able not only to enlarge to whatever size we require but also cropping out what is not required. Also if you plan to try to get some of your colour work published remember that publishers require transparencies and not prints or negatives from which to make reproductions for publication.

To make colour prints from slides you will need the following equipment much of which, if you are already doing your own black and white processing and printing, you should already have:

1 An enlarger with either a colour mixing head or a more simple enlarger with a filter drawer for which you will need a set of colour filters.
2 Masking frame.
3 Photographic thermometer.
4 Darkroom clock or timer.
5 Processing drum.
6 Three polythene or glass bottles for the processing solutions.
7 Measuring beakers.
8 Large glass or polythene container of at least two litres capacity in which to neutralise the used chemical solutions before pouring them away.
9 Protective rubber gloves to prevent contamination of hands when handling chemicals and chemical solutions.
10 Last, and most important, a darkroom that is completely lightproof.

A processing kit such as Cibachrome contains all the chemicals you will need – developer, bleach, fixers plus a neutraliser for the chemicals. Paper is bought separately.

You can use developing dishes for processing but this means that the whole of the processing (until the print is fixed) has to be done in complete darkness. If you use a processing drum once the paper has been exposed under the enlarger and then loaded into the drum the remainder of the processing routine can be carried out in daylight.

The most difficult aspect of colour work is filtration but this becomes easier the more you print and your eye will soon detect the various colour casts.

In making prints from transparencies or from a positive to a positive, exposure is the reverse of monochrome work. The less exposure the darker the picture, the more exposure the lighter the picture.

Also because the transparency gives a positive image on the enlarger baseboard it is much easier to compose than black and white where you use a negative image.

It is very important when you choose a transparency from which to make your first print that the transparency is sharp, correctly exposed and contains a good range of colours.

Like monochrome printing it is important first of all to make a test print. For this you will need a piece of card the same size as the print – say 10in x 8in. Cut out one quarter as in the sketch below.

In the introduction to this section I mentioned the Ilford 'Cibachrome'

Fig 5 Colour masking test card.

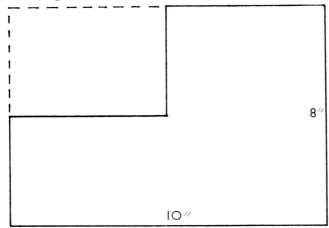

colour process and taken all round I think this is one of the simplest and best methods on the market at the moment for making prints from transparencies.

Simplified, the process is:
1 Mix the chemicals, including the water for rinsing, to the required temperature as in the instructions. Prepare the neutralising container (making sure it is clean and free of dust).
2 Put the selected slide in the enlarger and turn off the room lights.
3 Switch on enlarger and adjust to required format. Focus picture. Stop down lens by two stops and switch off enlarger.
4 Switch on the room light and according to the recommendations of the material place the appropriate basic filters with the UV absorbing filter into the enlarger filter tray or where appropriate set the required filter values on the colour head. *Now turn off the room light and do not turn on again until the exposed sheet is sealed in the processing drum.*
5 Remove Cibachrome printing paper from packet (sealing packet afterwards) and place in masking frame, emulsion side up. Place the exposure mask over the sheet of printing paper.
6 Make four test exposures using the exposure mask. Expose the first quarter of the picture for say 10 seconds. Turn the card and expose the second quarter

for 20 seconds, the third for 30 seconds and the last quarter for 40 seconds.
7 Place the exposed sheet in the processing drum, emulsion towards the inside, and close the drum.
8 Now switch on room light. Pour the required amount of developer into the drum and develop as per instructions. Agitate by rolling the drum back and forth on the bench for the total development time.
9 Pour out the developer into the neutralising container then pour in the rinse water and rinse for 30 seconds. Empty water into neutralising container and fill the drum with correct amount of bleach. Bleach for required time agitating the drum during bleaching.
10 Pour out bleach into neutralising container. Pour correct amount of fixer into the drum and fix for stated time. Agitate during fixing.
11 Pour out fixer into neutralising container.
12 Wash the print in the developing drum or flat in a dish for 3min in running water at a temperature of around 20°C. If the temperature is lower than this it will be necessary to wash the print for longer to ensure a good finish.
13 Dry the print with a hair dryer or leave to dry at room temperature.
14 Inspect test print and then make final print, processing as above.

Finished prints can be retouched with Cibachrome retouching dyes.

One final and very important point. Remember always to pour the used chemicals into the neutralising container before pouring away. The bleach solution is acid and therefore corrosive and if it is not neutralised will cause damage to the drainage system.

Addendum: Since writing the above the Cibachrome process has been slightly revised. The 'used' chemicals are now added together and neutralise themselves.

4
Railway Photography – General Principles

What makes a good railway photograph? Is it the location, lighting, time of year? All these and many more ingredients will help to produce a picture that has atmosphere and interest, and one which will hold the viewer's attention. All these aspects will be discussed in later chapters. But here I want to deal specifically with the basis of general railway photography, that is the photographic approach to the different types of traction (large or small). I have divided them into the following categories:

    (a) Steam
    (b) Diesel
    (c) Electric
    (d) Miniature

To obtain interesting photographs of any type of traction certain problems and peculiarities present themselves to the photographer and once you know how to approach and overcome them you should then have a good basis from which to produce interesting pictures. Once this basic standard has been achieved it opens the door to far more creative things (which will also be discussed in detail later on).

Steam

The magic of steam! A great many people would assume that you have only to point the camera at a steam engine, press the shutter release and 'hey presto', a master shot. This is not the case – far from it. Many people would agree that in most cases the very essence of a good steam action picture is for the locomotive to be throwing out smoke and steam; thus the first basic rule is, if at all possible, to take your picture from a location where you know that the engine will be working hard, as for example on a steep incline, or leaving a

station or speed restricted section. Having said that, remember that there are occasions when the locations and lighting conditions are so photogenic that they can compensate for the lack of exhaust from the locomotive.

As steam engines come in all shapes and sizes it follows that certain photographic angles suit certain engines. Some engines may photograph better from a low angle looking up at them but with other types they may be more photogenic from above. And of course the photographer will have his own particular favourite angles for different engines. For example, I like to photograph the A4 Pacific from a low viewpoint because I feel that it has a very powerful streamlined front end which, when photographed from this angle (especially with a good exhaust), gives a feeling of power and speed which are essentials of any good action photograph. The opposite I feel is true when photographing *King George V*. Here the graceful lines of Great Western engines are shown to best advantage when taken from above.

It does not always work out like this. There are many times when the location itself dictates the angle from which you photograph the locomotive. For example when photographing around the Diggle and Standedge area (on the Manchester – Huddersfield – Leeds route) which abounds in beautiful, wild photogenic scenery, the landscape cries out to be included in your picture which means that regardless of the type of locomotive the best approach is to photograph from above. Remember though that in some hill or mountain locations if the line is above the valley floor crossing a river, for example, a

camera level at or below line level may make the scene more dramatic or might be necessary in order to get a natural hill or mountain top skyline within the camera frame. But in general, when in ordinary surroundings where there is little if any outstanding scenery (and in practice, many locations are like this), the locomotive becomes the dominant part of the composition. In these situations it is worth experimenting with photographic angles to achieve as photogenic a picture as is possible.

Another very important point to remember, and this applies when photographing any type of traction, is that when you are taking action photographs it is important to use a shutter speed fast enough to freeze the train in action. If your shutter speed is too slow this usually results in movement or blur on the front end of the locomotive making an unsatisfactory picture. For example, if it is a bright day with plenty of light and you have a medium speed film in your camera of say around 125ASA and assuming you are using a standard lens on your camera, you should have a meter reading giving a shutter speed of a 1/500th sec with a lens aperture of around f5·6 to f8. This shutter speed should enable you to freeze most trains in action and to get a reasonably wide angle on the subject. In the case of HSTs, electrics and diesel expresses it would be advisable to increase the shutter speed to 1/1000th sec and open the lens aperture to f4 or f5·6, or alternatively stay on the previous camera setting (1/500th at f5·6 to f8) and narrow the angle to freeze the movement of the train. On the other hand if it is a dull day (as is so often the case!) with a meter reading of a 1/250th sec at f2·8 to f4 you need to narrow the angle to slow the relative movement of the train in order to stop the action. In other words the faster the train and/or the wider the angle from which you take your photograph the higher the shutter speed required. The slower the train and/or the narrower the angle of the picture it is then possible to use a slower shutter speed and still freeze the action.

Another point to bear in mind when taking action photographs is that the greater the distance that the camera is away from the train the less is the movement, which enables you to use a slower shutter speed and smaller lens aperture (giving greater focal length). The nearer you are to the train the relative movement is greater, which means that you need a faster shutter speed to freeze the action. At the same time by increasing your shutter speed you must open up the lens to a wider aperture (which decreases the focal length).

In circumstances where it is really dull and you are down to 1/125th sec at f2·8, it might be worthwhile trying either a panned shot (see chapter five) or, (mainly in the case of steam locomotives) what is known as a three-quarter rear shot. This simply means photographing the locomotive as it is going away from you. This is because as the movement is away from you it can be stopped with a slower shutter speed because with the locomotive at the far end of the train, its relative movement is reduced. It is worthwhile trying this type of shot in normal circumstances and not only in dull lighting conditions. Many interesting railway photographs have been taken from this angle but it could be a mistake to regard it as a second shot to be taken as an extra after the normal first shot which is usually a three-quarter front view of the train. If you want a really good 'going away shot' it is far better to concentrate on that alone, and achieve what you require rather than taking a snatched shot hoping that it will turn out to be a good one (that is unless you are using a motor drive which should give a you chance of good shots both ways).

A final word of caution on the use of shutter speeds in action photography. Try to avoid using shutter speeds of less than 1/250th sec (with the exception of panned and 'going away shots') because it is doubtful if a 1/125th or certainly 1/60th sec would stop a train even almost head-on, and at the same time when using speeds as slow as 1/60th you may start to encounter camera shake.

Another problem that arises from time to time when photographing steam locomotives is when they are facing tender or bunker (in the case of tank engines) first. Unlike locomotives facing forward (smoke box first) it is pointless to take them head on or from too narrow an angle otherwise all we shall get in our pictures is a photograph of a tender or bunker. In these circumstances we need to take as wide an angle as we can (shutter speed permitting) and from reasonable distance in order to get a good side view of the engine and train in a landscape setting which in turn should make for a more interesting picture.

Diesel

I think it would be fair to say that on the whole the diesel locomotive is not as obviously photogenic as its steam counterpart. This in itself most certainly provides a challenge to the photographer of modern traction.

Unlike steam where a good exhaust alone can make an atmospheric picture, when photographing diesel traction you need to make as much use of lighting and location as is possible in order to create atmosphere. And that is where you have a decided advantage in Britain when photographing diesel trains as opposed to steam. Unlike steam trains which only run on certain days on certain specific BR routes and preserved lines, diesel trains are running seven days a week the length and breadth of the country. In consequence you are more or less able to choose the sort

Steam hard at work in a classical setting is well portrayed in this shot of Jubilee class 4–6–0 No 5690 *Leander* climbing near Ais Gill summit with the SLOA southbound Cumbrian Mountain Express. The precise location is Ais Gill viaduct and the date 28 January 1982.

Camera, Nikon FM fitted with 35mm medium wide angle lens plus yellow filter. Exposure 1/250th second at f3·5. Film, Ilford XP1 (rated at 400ASA), developed in XP1 chemicals.
The dull conditions which meant using a fairly wide aperture warranted the use of a medium wide angle lens with its greater depth of field and at the same time no distortion is discernable. It will also be noted that as the train was not travelling fast 1/250th sec shutter speed was sufficient to freeze the action.

of lighting and locations which should lead to good atmospheric pictures. This is well borne out by the many fine photographs to be seen today in books and magazines on modern traction.

At certain angles, as with steam locomotives, some types of diesels look better than others. I always feel that a Deltic is more photogenic when photographed from a low angle, accentuating the aggressive-looking front end and giving a genuine impression of a powerful locomotive at work. But again the photographer will have his own favourite angles for different types of locomotive, and with any type of traction it is well worth experimenting to find the most photogenic angles.

The lack of exhaust in diesels (at least in the best maintained examples) can be made up to a certain extent by use of a good sky effect. Unlike steam you can pick your day and moment when photographing modern traction. Wait until you have a good sunny day with plenty of white fluffy clouds, fit a yellow or red filter to your camera lens (if taking black and white) and go out and try your hand. You will be surprised at the effect and impact a good cloud effect can have on your composition, adding life and atmosphere.

Another good effect with which to create atmosphere in a modern traction picture is to photograph the train as it tilts away from you on a curve. This gives an impression of imbalance and so, movement. Experiment with lighting conditions, especially early morning and evening when you have low sunlight. Tremendous lighting effects (which of course can add great impact to your pictures) can be created especially when taking your photographs with extreme back lighting *(contre-jour)* and so getting a golden glow on the side of the train. These are commonly known as 'glint shots'. (See chapter six for further technical details). Splendid effects can also be obtained in winter especially when there is a sprinkling of snow around, but more about that in a later chapter.

Another effective way to photograph modern traction (or any type of traction for that matter) is the reflection shot. This simply means that you mirror the locomotive or train in water so that your picture consists of the actual locomotive and train plus its reflected image. If you are taking station or shed shots the reflection could be in a pool of water created by a sudden shower or if you are out in the country or near the coast good reflections are possible when the train is crossing over a river/stream or estuary. But the water must be fairly calm otherwise you will not get a good reflection so obviously avoid wet and windy days for this type of picture.

Make as much use of locations as is possible. There are many fine viaducts, bridges, stations, signal-boxes, semaphore signals, etc, to incorporate into your picture. Remember when photographing modern traction you can more or less choose the weather and to a great extent the location – remembering of course to avoid trespassing.

Electric
Most of the points mentioned in the diesel section apply almost equally well when photographing electric traction, especially third rail. But with overhead catenary certain obvious problems present themselves and you should be fairly selective when photographing this type of electric traction from above, but there is plenty of scope for good electric traction photographs when taken from the side and three-quarter front and rear. This is especially so when they are photographed from a reasonable distance and therefore incorporated into the landscape. For example make use of trees to frame the picture or maybe a river or flooded field in order to create a strong foreground. The catenary masts themselves, with their receding pattern also provide a strong visual feature which can be made to enhance a photograph. All these and many more things will help to make far more interesting photographs of what is not an easy

6 June 1981. A southbound DMU crosses the High Level bridge at Newcastle with an evening local train. The evening light accentuates the structures of the bridge as well as the train and the surrounding features which make for a harmonious composition.

This train could have been photographed a few feet further on but by shooting at this position the arch of the bridge leads the eye to the front of the train.

This type of setting is very photogenic for any type of traction but even more so when photographing modern traction, the lighting and location with repeating bridge patterns providing the dramatic interest.

Camera, Nikon FM with 85mm lens plus yellow filter. Exposure 1/250th sec at f5·6. Film, Ilford FP4 (rated at 160ASA), developed in Aculux.

This is the standard three-quarter front shot as applied to overhead electric traction. The tilt of the locomotive on the cant of the curve helps to provide an impression of movement and the framing of the train with the catenary provides a more balanced picture.

The location is Milford, south of Stafford, and the train is a southbound freight hauled by Class 86 locomotive No 86032, 15 April 1982.

Camera, Nikon FM with 85mm lens plus yellow filter. Exposure 1/1000th sec at f6·3. Film, Ilford XP1, developed in XP1 chemicals.

This picture is an example of how you can use natural surroundings to frame the locomotive and by taking from a side view using the frame (in this case trees) to cut out the catenary masts etc. It is important that when taking trains from this angle, especially as in this case with the train travelling at high speed, a very fast shutter speed is essential.

A 135mm lens (in 35mm size) was deliberately used in this instance to keep the foreground blurred and the train reasonably sharp, focusing the attention on the subject.

The location is Norton Bridge Junction, north of Stafford. The train is a northbound Inter-City hauled by Class 86 No 86231, on 15 April 1982.

Camera, Nikon FM with 135mm lens. Exposure 1/1000th sec at f6·3. Film, Ilford XP1 (400 ASA), developed in XP1 chemicals.

subject to tackle. Certainly photographing overhead electric traction is a challenge to the railway photographer but one that can be overcome with a certain amount of thought and of course experiment.

Miniature Railways
Miniature railways, and by miniature I mean railways of 15in gauge or less, are often neglected by the railway photographer, much to his detriment, I feel. In Britain alone there are many splendid lines of various gauges spread throughout the country. They have many fine examples of British and overseas locomotives, mostly working steam models as well as many freelance designs. Many of the railways are situated in highly photogenic locations such as parks or woodland and

50

some have fine railway buildings, signals, bridges, etc, all of which can contribute to better railway photography. Some of the 15in gauge lines like the Romney, Hythe & Dymchurch in South East England and the Ravenglass & Eskdale in the Lake District, were built as a means of transport for the local population, as opposed to the tourist lines which they are today.

There are two major ways in which to approach miniature railway photography. Because of the size of the locomotives and trains you can deliberately include people such as the driver and passengers (especially children) in your picture and make them part of the railway scene, thus giving your photographs the true scale of miniature railways. This is probably much the best way to photograph the smallest gauges. But it is also possible to approach 15in gauge railways from the other angle, that is, to try and make the locomotives and trains appear as if they were standard gauge.

Obviously this second approach is far from easy but by careful and thoughtful photography it is possible on occasions to make the little ones look like their big brothers on the main line. One way to approach this would be to photograph a train almost head on as it pulls out of a station and if the exhaust is strong enough it should obscure the driver and any passengers. But make sure that the background is something like trees or bushes so that the size of the train is not given away as it would be if for example you took it against a background of houses.

Another method that can be used but which requires some patience on the part of the photographer is to wait until a train has discharged its passengers at a terminus station and the driver has gone off for a quick break and then, without people around to give away the scale of the locomotive and train plus a bit of ingenuity and luck, it is possible to obtain a more main line type of picture.

One very important point to remember is that because of their obviously smaller size, you will have to be that much nearer to get a balanced picture, in which case, you will need to use a small aperture (high f number) in order to get a good depth of field. If you are photographing a locomotive from, say, 6ft and you use too large an aperture (low f number) you will find the front of the locomotive sharp, but the back end out of focus, with any coaches behind as a blur.

But however you approach the photography of miniature railways, you will be amazed by the sheer beauty of the locomotives and their likeness to their big brothers on the main line, by the care and attention given them by their enthusiastic owners and, last but not least, by the enjoyment they bring to many thousands of people, young and old alike. It all helps to make photographing these little beauties so rewarding and such a pleasure.

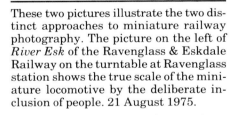

These two pictures illustrate the two distinct approaches to miniature railway photography. The picture on the left of *River Esk* of the Ravenglass & Eskdale Railway on the turntable at Ravenglass station shows the true scale of the miniature locomotive by the deliberate inclusion of people. 21 August 1975.

Camera, Nikkormat with 50mm lens plus yellow filter. Exposure 1/500th sec at f8. Film, Ilford FP4 rated at 200ASA and developed in Acuspecial.

The scene on the right is a deliberate attempt to convey the opposite impression. By getting more of the front end view and from a fairly low angle, coupled with an exhaust that hides the driver, the impression is almost one of the main line. But for shots like this you do need luck especially as in this case with the exhaust.
Picture details: Romney, Hythe & Dymchurch No 10 *Dr Syn* pulls out of Hythe, 30 March 1975.

Camera, Nikkormat with 85mm lens plus yellow filter. Exposure 1/500th sec at f8. Film, Ilford FP4 (rated at 200ASA), developed in Acuspecial.

5

Style,
Composition
and Techniques

Style

With all art forms (and I certainly regard photography as an art form) there is usually more than one approach or style, and railway photography is certainly no exception. Being also a musician with a love of jazz I find that railway photography like jazz can be divided into three distinct approaches, traditional, mainstream and modern.

The style of the traditional approach can be described simply as the classic three-quarter front view of the locomotive and train in action with the accent on the train rather than the scenery and surroundings. This style was very much the hallmark of such early railway photographers as the Rev T. B. Parley and Dr T. F. Budden and perfected by F. E. Mackay and H. Gordon Tidey. A glance through *The Railway Magazine* of the period between 1910 and the late 1920s will show many fine examples of this approach. But as I mentioned in the introduction photographers of this period were very much limited by their heavy and cumbersome equipment and it was only at the end of the 1920s and early 1930s that styles began to change.

There were a number of reasons for this but principal among them was the advent of smaller and very much lighter cameras using roll film instead of plates.

A new style thus emerged which I have called the mainstream approach. This used the best of the older traditional style, that is, good sharp pictures of trains in action still usually with a three-quarter front viewpoint but using a very much more pictorial approach to the subject, incorporating in the picture far more of the railway and surrounding scenery.

Since its inception the pictorial approach has remained with us as a leading style in railway photography. And why not? It incorporates both old and new and for a lot of people it would seem to convey the very essence and atmosphere of the railway scene. But we must not turn our backs on anything new. Certainly the modern or New Approach (as it became popularly known) to railway photography and pioneered by Colin Gifford, John Hunt, Ian Krause and others in the 1960s added an exciting and very realistic dimension to the medium.

With this approach the accent is on the whole railway scene and in many instances the train is of lesser significance in relation to the scene depicted in the photograph. A good example would be a picture of a freight train passing through its natural industrial environment, a scene full of factories, chimneys, smoke, etc; by putting the accent on the industrial scene as a whole and not just the train this should in turn convey the impression of a freight in its natural settings.

Another example of the modern style is to photograph men at work. It could be a booking clerk, shunter, driver, signalman or a host of other people who work on the railways. Also passengers can make very interesting studies and the New Approach has certainly been a pioneer in the human involvement in the railway scene. But a word of warning. To capture this type of picture you have sometimes only a few seconds in which to work. A delay and the magic moment may have gone by. It is never quite the same if people pose for photographs. There is nearly always an air of self-consciousness about 'posed' pictures.

This modern approach certainly

seems to fit in well when photographing modern traction giving added impetus to what in some cases could be a rather flat subject. Generally this type of photography calls for more creative thought on the part of the cameraman, which in many cases should produce pictures of an imaginative and creative nature. Very often photographs are taken with what can be called 'available light,' that is minimum or poor natural light, which with fast films can achieve presentable results even inside buildings without flash. A gloomy interior of an engine shed could really be captured as it really was.

To conclude this section on the different approaches to railway photography the three main styles can be summarised:

(a) Traditional.
This style of railway photography is basically a three-quarter front view of the locomotive and train, mainly to the exclusion of the surroundings etc but very useful to give an impact picture of a train hard at work — particularly steam — and of course when the surroundings do not warrant too much inclusion in the picture, it requires good photographic technique (as indeed do all styles) to execute properly.

(b) Mainstream.
This middle of the road or pictorial approach has much to offer and allows the photographer plenty of scope in his compositions. It certainly seems to be a very useful style for depicting the steam scene.

(c) Modern.
This New Approach allows the photographer freedom of expression and creativity, and would arguably

seem to be very suitable when applied to modern traction.

All of these styles have much to offer the railway photographer and should form a firm base on which he can then build his own individual ideas and possibly one day help to create a style of his own.

Composition.
By composition we mean the lines which draw the eye to the focus of interest, and give a feeling of balance to the picture. We often choose a location for a photograph with an intuitive sense of composition, which is in fact developed over years of looking at famous works of art and good quality photographs in advertising. Often we perceive a master shot without being aware of the mechanics of the composition, and select the stance and lens to achieve it. Sometimes, of course, the situation is far from ideal; other photographers may have got there

first and courtesy demands that the latecomer does not obstruct their view. Sometimes the train comes early and catches the photographer unprepared; the resulting snatched shot can sometimes be turned into an exciting composition by means of careful cropping.

We should study the paintings of the great masters of the Renaissance and after, for it was in this period that artists came to grips with the problems of perspective and foreshortening, using a viewing device known as the 'camera obscura'. This was a box with a lens at the front and a mirror within, which transmitted the landscape onto a baseboard, albeit very dimly, where the artist could mark out the scene. Every artist had his recognisable style, as indeed have great photographers, but all depended on a limited number of constructions which were acceptable to the public. Rubens is famous for his curves – or

The picture above of Class A2 Pacific No 60532 *Blue Peter* near Plean Junction on 18 June 1966 with an Aberdeen – Glasgow express is a traditional three-quarter front style of picture. Although the train dominates the scene the features of the locomotive and the exhaust make up for the lack of scenery.

Camera, Konica range-finder with 45mm lens plus yellow filter. Exposure 1/500th sec at f4. Film, Kodak Plus X (125ASA), developed in D76 (undiluted).

perhaps for his curvaceous forms. The Dutch painter Hobbema is famous for his view down a straight road lined with tall trees, an ideal example of the use of perspective. In this section I shall demonstrate some of these popular constructions, and illustrate them with photographs.

It was the French painter Ingres who held the opinion that 'Drawing includes everything except the tint.' Although this takes little account of the emotional impact of the use of colour, dealt with in the section on colour photography, it underlines the importance of good composition. No picture will be satisfying unless it fulfils certain requirements, relying on either linear structure or repeated rhythms of shape and pattern, or as generally happens, a combination of several aspects.

(a) The Golden Section. This was discovered by the Ancient Greeks, and this proportional ratio was used throughout the temple buildings on the Acropolis. The relationship of the parts is expressed by the formula $\frac{a}{b} = \frac{b}{(a+b)}$ or approximately 1 : 1·6 as can be seen in the diagram fig 6. In practice this means that the most interesting place for your locomotive is just off centre in the photograph. By following the rule of the Golden Section there is a choice of four positions, as indicated by the extra dotted lines. In most conventional railway photography, the point chosen would be one of the two lower positions, because the photographer often stands up on a bank or bridge and looks down on the train. But if he were looking upwards, then one of the upper positions would probably be his choice. It should be noted that when photographing steam engines, the focus of interest falls behind the smokebox door and underneath the chimney, not on the buffer beam, as the directional lines often run through the exhaust leading the eye to that part of the engine. If the photographer takes liberties with this proportion then there must be a good reason. The dramatic tension must be balanced by some compen-

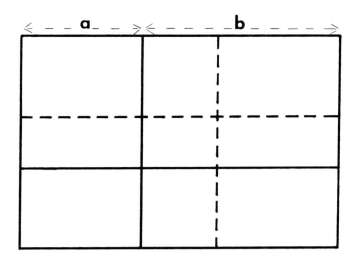

Fig 6 The rectangle divided by the Golden Sections into four possible focal points of interest.

sating factor, such as a very powerful exhaust, or significant detail in the foreground.

(b) Starburst, from a vanishing point. This structure is frequently met in the railway scene, when a train is either approaching or departing. This static scene is given dramatic interest by placing the mysteriously-hidden destination well to the right of centre. The low viewpoint helps to make the roof-line slope more steeply, a trick which stimulates a feeling of movement. Notice the reflections in the high gloss of the carriage to the right, without which the shadows would be much too heavy, and notice too how the wiggly lines are

repeated in the cable on the ground, fig 7.

(c) The Triangle. This is often found on railways because the parallel lines of the rails and rolling stock, following the rules of perspective, slope towards the vanishing point in the distance. This is very clear in fig 8 with the upper side of the triangle following an invisible line through the tilt of the driver's cap. This tiny detail, perceived unconsciously, is so important to the composition, and guides the photographer's finger to press the shutter NOW and not two seconds later. Notice that the secondary focus of interest, where the driver emerges from the cab, falls on the top right

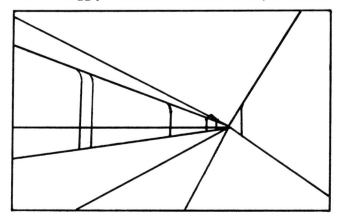

Fig 7 Perspective lines converging on a vanishing point.

A pair of class 25s, Nos 25062 and 25027 wait to leave Bewdley (Severn Valley Railway) on the morning of 31 October 1981 with the SVR Cathedrals Express to Paddington via Worcester and Oxford.

Camera, Zeiss Super Ikonta 531 – 16, 6 x 6cm folding camera with 75mm lens. Exposure 1/100th sec at f5·6. Film, Ilford FP4 (125ASA), developed in I D11 (undiluted).

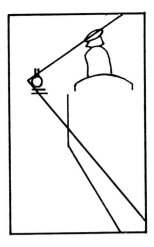

Fig 8

Fig 9

Golden Section. In fig 9 the triangle lies on the chimney (apex) and buffer beam (base) but the points of the triangle are completed by the two railway staff, particularly by the one with the bent leg. This is another critical moment for shutter release. Notice that the object of the inspector's interest falls on the Golden Section. This picture is also enhanced by the repeating rhythm of circles.

Povoa, Northern Portugal, 20 September 1974. Metre gauge 2–6–0 tank No 103 gets the final once over before leaving with the 12.32 to Porto.

Camera, Nikkormat with 50mm lens plus yellow filter. Exposure 1/500th sec at f5·6. Film, Ilford FP4 (rated at 200ASA), developed in Acuspecial.

Fairbourne Railway near Barmouth (15in gauge), 8 August 1973. Trains hauled by *Katie* and *Sian* about to pass each other at the crossing loop.

Camera, Nikkormat with 50mm lens plus yellow filter. Exposure 1/250th sec at f8. Film, Ilford FP4 (rated at 200ASA), developed in Acuspecial.

(d) Dynamic Diagonals. Sloping lines tend to create a feeling of movement. In fig 10 the banked camber of the bend naturally tilts the locomotive, and gives it extra punch as it snorts out of the cutting. It follows that a good place to catch an engine at speed is head-on coming round a bend. (This position helps to freeze the movement if the photographer cannot use a fast shutter speed). Some stations are built on a curving track, which is banked for non-stop expresses. A static shot by a platform can be given extra life by catching the engine in a tilted position. In fig 11 a slanted viewpoint has turned all parallels and right angles into diagonals. Notice the slope of the cage that holds the mailbags, how it carries the eye to the pointing finger.

Vale of Rheidol Railway 2–6–2 tank No 9 *Prince of Wales* approaches Devil's Bridge station on 9 August 1973 with a train from Aberystwyth.

Camera, Nikkormat with 50mm lens plus yellow filter. Exposure 1/250th sec at f2·8. Film, Ilford FP4 (rated at 200 ASA), developed in Acuspecial.

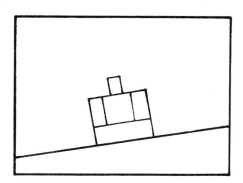

Fig 10

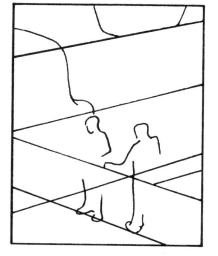

Fig 11

Crew change at York. Peak class diesel locomotive on northbound train, 23 May 1981.

Camera, Nikon FM with 50mm lens. Exposures 1/125th sec at f4. Film, Ilford FP4 (rated at 160ASA), developed in Aculux.

The famous Vordenberg incline in Southern Austria, 28 August 1974. A pair of 97 class rack locomotive (Nos 97–209 and 97–201) near Vordenberg to Markt with iron ore empties.

Camera, Nikkormat with 85mm lens plus yellow filter. Exposure 1/250th sec at f8. Film, Ilford FP4 (rated at 160ASA), developed in Acutol.

DB 012 Pacific No 012 055 near Meppen (West Germany) with an Emden–Rheine Express, 21 March 1975.

Camera, Nikkormat with 85mm lens plus yellow filter. Exposure 1/1000th sec at f5·6. Film, Ilford FP4 (rated at 200ASA), developed in Acuspecial.

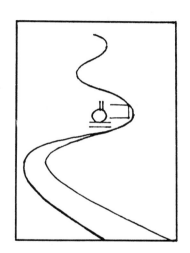

Fig 12

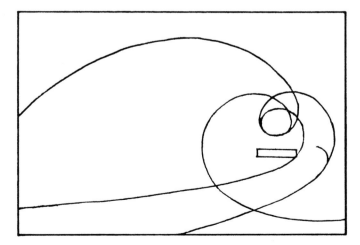

Fig 13

(e) The Hogarth Spiral, or Vertical Spiral. The painter Hogarth developed this device for composing society portraits of ladies in crinolines and wide-brimmed hats. This lends itself very naturally to views down reverse curves, finished off with trees or billowing exhausts, fig 12.

(f) Flat Spirals. This location was chosen to display the plume of smoke to the greatest advantage. In fig 13 the spirals in the top half run in opposite directions to those in the lower half, creating extra interest. If the wind had been blowing from the other side, the curves would have interlocked forming a whirlpool effect. Notice the importance of the shadow in the foreground, bringing the eye into the subject, and how the clump of trees helps to carry the line of the rails round the corner.

(g) The layered effect, fig 14. This setting for *Sir Nigel Gresley* was chosen for the repeating rhythms of the trees, the railway line occupying the Golden Section at the bottom. Layered lines can often be found in places like estuaries or in cloud formations. In this instance the A4 met a Class 40 in the chosen spot. The shape of this fortunate encounter was echoed in the break in the line of trees in the middle distance.

(h) Contrast. In fig 15 the layered effect is elaborated by a vertical grid of poplar trees. This is a useful device on two counts. First, on a grey day with little variation in the middle tones, the photographer needs as much contrast as possible, supplied here by the dark tree trunks against the light sky. Second, whenever an object is veiled it becomes more intriguing; the movement of the train behind the boles is a trick to catch the attention. There is also a triangular structure running upwards through the steam and downwards into the weeping willow. In fig 16, the famous

Class A4 Pacific No 4498 *Sir Nigel Gresley* on the southbound Cumbrian Mountain Express meets Class 40 diesel locomotive No 40194 on a northbound goods. The location is just north of Culgaith on the Settle & Carlisle line and the date 15 July 1981.

Camera, Nikon FM with 85mm lens plus yellow filter. Exposure 1/500th sec at f5·6. Film, Ilford FP4 (rated at 160ASA), developed in Aculux.

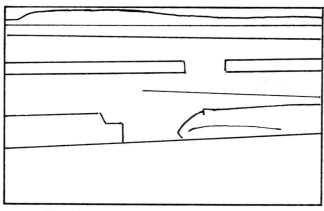

Fig 14

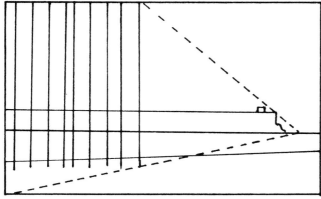

Fig 15

LMS Jubilee 4–6–0 *Leander* pulls out of Bridgnorth (Severn Valley Railway) for Hampton Loade on 21 November 1981.

This picture also serves as a good example of what you can achieve in poor lighting conditions. Because there was insufficient light to get a satisfactory three-quarter front position (it would have meant an exposure of 250th second at around f2 which might have frozen the action but there would have been very little depth of field) I decided to try for a going away shot in which case the shutter speed of 125th second was sufficient to freeze the action and the aperture of f3 gave a better depth of field resulting in a pleasant composition.

Camera, Nikon FM with 50mm lens. Exposure 1/125th sec at f3. Film, Ilford XP1 (rated at 400ASA), developed in XP1 chemicals.

diamond crossing at Newcastle, photographed here from the castle battlements, is the setting for an HST. Visually the IC125 units do not change and demand resourcefulness on the part of the cameraman to find an original treatment. Here the contrast is provided by the sparkling texture of the crossing lines behind the smooth streamlining of the HST. This picture also contains the elements of the Golden Section, and the rhythm of the canopies echoing the curve of the cab and guiding lines from such features as the retaining wall and the island platforms.

A northbound HST pulls out of New-castle Central on 6 June 1981. Note the detail in the shadow area which has been retained by holding back during the printing stage.

Camera, Nikon FM 85mm lens plus yellow filter. Exposure 1/250th sec at f6·3. Film, Ilford FP4 (rated at 160ASA), developed in Aculux.

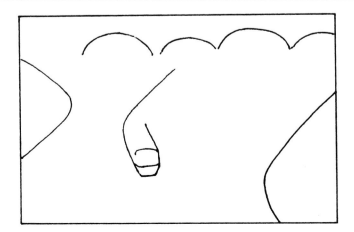

Fig 16

(i) The Square and the Circle. This most photogenic of stations, Kings Cross, once host to A4s as remembered in that famous view through a side arch, is here the setting for a brace of Deltics, now also but a memory. In fig 17 the squareness of the yellow fronts makes a geometric contrast with the circular span of the canopy. This type of composition lends itself well to head-on views of steam engines with side tanks or smoke deflectors, or diesels coming under bridges. A little assymetry brings the right hand Deltic onto the Golden Section. These locomotives illustrate the previous remarks on textured backgrounds for plain shapes, and their cab windows repeat the circular rhythms of the roof girders.

Deltics locomotives Nos D55019 *Tulyar* and D55009 *Alycidon* make a splendid sight as they pose in the platforms at Kings Cross, 20 June 1981.

Camera, Nikon FM with 35mm lens. Exposure 1/60th sec at f4. Film, Ilford Pan F (rated at 50ASA), developed in I D11 (undiluted). Note the beautiful tonal quality of this film.

Fig 17

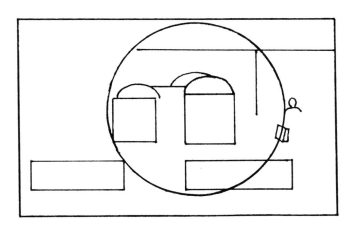

(j) Repeated Shapes. As in some of the previous examples, an outstanding feature is given far more meaning if it is put in a setting of sympathetic shapes, fig 18. This locomotive has two domes of an interesting outline. Fortunately I spotted a piece of waste ground smoothed by passing feet into mounds of a similar shape, and caught the engine as it was passing this place. Shapes can be repeated in reflections, as when an engine crosses a river bridge, or passes a lake.

Turkish Railway 2–10–2 No 57016 near Torbali Junction with a Denizli to Izmir train, 23 February 1976.

Camera, Nikkormat with 50mm lens plus yellow filter. Exposure 1/500th sec at f5·6. Film, Ilford FP4 (rated at 160 ASA), developed in Aculux.

Fig 18

(k) Filling the picture, when the train is distant. It sometimes happens that the photographer cannot get near enough to the train to fill the frame, and needs something extra to complete the scene. One obvious solution is to use the repeated rhythm, as in fig 19 where the caravans duplicate the shape of the carriages, and the headland echoes the shape of the smoke. In the second picture, fig 20, not only does the tree fill the sky with an interesting silhouette, but the direction of its branches is similar to the slant of the exhaust. The tree also reflects the spartan appearance of the industrial railway scene.

4472 *Flying Scotsman* climbs near Goodrington with a Paignton–Kingswear train (Torbay Steam Railway), 21 July 1973.

Camera, Nikkormat with 85mm lens plus yellow filter. Exposure 1/250th sec at f8. Film, Ilford FP4 (rated at 200ASA), developed in Acuspecial.

Note the use of a short telephoto lens in this shot which slightly foreshortens the background and thus emphasises it.

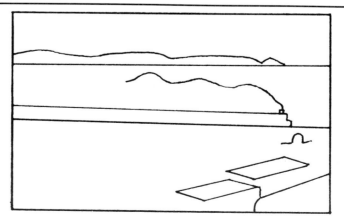

Fig 19

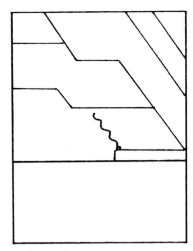

Fig 20

Left. Littleton Colliery (Staffs), 2 January 1969. Littleton No 2, 0–6–0 saddle tank between Penkridge and Boscomoor with empties for the colliery.

Camera, Konica 35mm range-finder fitted with a 45mm lens plus yellow filter. Exposure 1/125th sec at f5·6. Film, Kodak Plus X (rated at 125ASA), developed in D76 (undiluted).

Right. Bickershaw Colliery near Leigh, Lancashire, 21 June 1972. 0–6–0 saddle tank *Spitfire* heads for the exchange sidings with loaded wagons.

Camera, Nikkormat with 50mm lens plus yellow filter. Exposure 1/125th sec at f11. Film, Kodak Plus X (rated 125ASA), developed in D 76 (undiluted).

(l) Framing the picture. In a similar way to the previous landscape, photographers often try to include branches to fill the tops of their compositions. This device helps to frame the subject like curtains on a stage. It is fairly easy to find doorways and windows in an engine shed, or in signalboxes, to surround your view of your engine. By keeping your mind open to the unexpected, and being prepared to climb up or crouch down, you may find some novel way of achieving

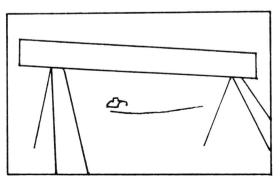

Fig 21

this. In fig 21, this buffer at the end of a siding makes a window for those prepared to bend their knees. Notice how the slopes of the buttressing girders help to lead the eye onto the train. There are plenty of other useful structures such as signals, the yellow cutout numbers on posts, the lattice work in bridges and brackets. Sometimes it is the gap between familiar objects which takes on an unexpected shape, such as between the buffers and pipes of the carriage couplings. In fig 22 the engine is framed in the tunnel of girders of this South African bridge, and carries an air of pent-up energy. Notice also how the circle of the boiler is contained in the square of the webbing, and how the engine falls on the Golden Section.

Fig 22

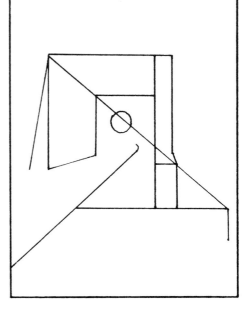

Overleaf: South African Railways Class 25 4–8–4 No 3403 near Ficksburg with a Bloemfontein-Bethlehem train, 3 August 1981.

Camera, Nikon FM with 50mm lens plus yellow filter. Exposure 1/250th sec at f8. Film, Ilford FP4 (rated at 125ASA), developed in I D11 (undiluted).

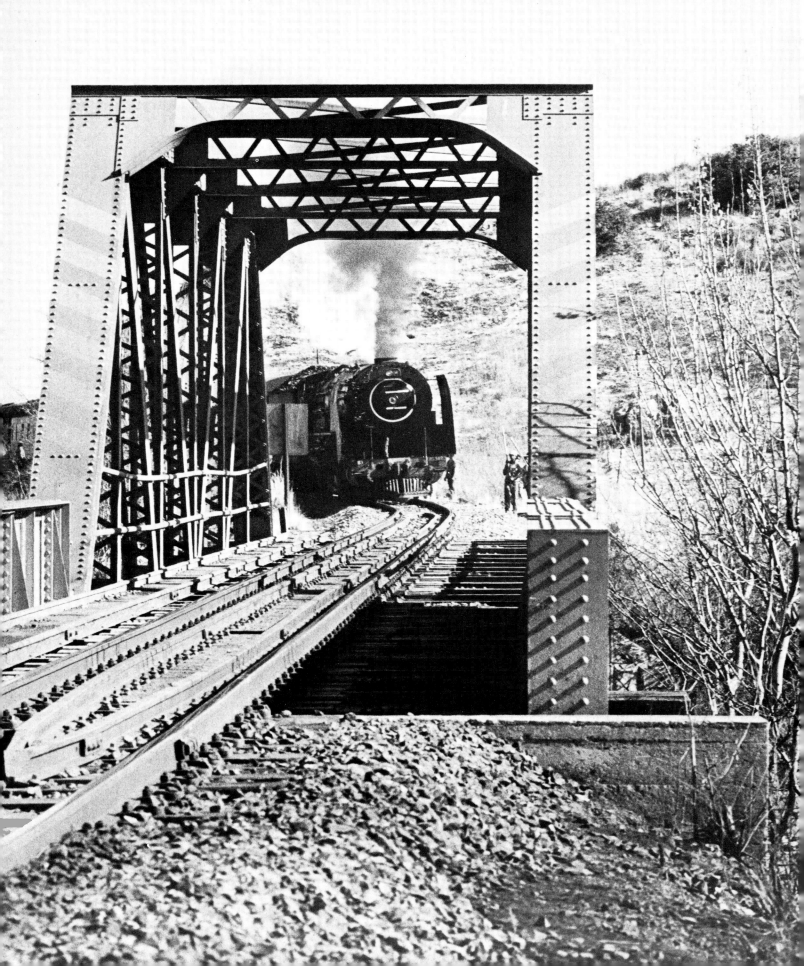

Technique

This section deals with the techniques required for the many different types of pictures that the photographer is able to achieve within the medium of railway photography.

(a) Landscapes

The landscape is probably the most common form of railway photograph yet in many ways it is one of the most difficult type of picture in which to achieve success. The biggest fault with most landscape pictures is one of trying to get too much of the landscape into the shot, so that you finish up with the train virtually lost in the panorama. Thus it is important to keep a balance between the train and scenery unless there are exceptional features or circumstances which dictate otherwise.

A medium telephoto lens can be an asset when you are unable to get near enough to the scene to get the right balance. But if you use a lens that is too long you get a certain amount of foreshortening which may distort and spoil the picture.

When you are unable to obtain the right sort of balance in your picture one idea is to frame the train with an interesting foreground feature such as a tree, gate or fence etc. This will not only add to the character of the scene but spotlight the train.

This picture well illustrates a balanced landscape. Strong characteristic foreground interest is combined with mountainous backdrop (emphasised by the use of a short telephoto lens). Added to this is the strong cloud effect brought about by the use of a yellow filter. The brilliant sunlight enabled me to use a small aperture (with a fast shutter speed) which meant a generous depth of field. Note that everything is in focus, from the house to the hills. Also note that the size of the engine is well in proportion to the overall picture.

This beautiful location is Bull Gill south of Kirkby Stephen on the Settle & Carlisle line. The train is the southbound Cumbrian Mountain Express hauled by Pacific No 34092 *City of Wells* and the date 3 May 1982.

Camera, Nikon FM with 85mm lens and yellow filter. Exposure 1/500th sec at f9. Film, Ilford XP1, rated 400ASA and developed in XP1 chemicals.

The inclusion of the row of neat terraced houses in this picture certainly gives the impression of a train at work in urban surroundings, in this case just west of Stalybridge station; the train is the northbound Trans Pennine Pullman hauled by Jubilee class 4–6–0 No 5690 *Leander* on 10 April 1982.

Camera, Nikon FM with 85mm lens plus yellow filter. Exposure 1/500th sec at f5·6. Film, Ilford XP1 (rated at 400ASA), developed in XP1 chemicals.

(b) Towns and Cities

The industrial landscape that can be created in towns and cities obviously differs from the rural landscape mentioned earlier. But it is just as important to get the right balance between the train and its urban or industrial surroundings as when you are photographing country landscapes and the same rules apply although the surroundings are considerably different.

To get the feel of town or city in your picture it is important to include things that denote this. For example a row of neat terraced houses would perhaps give the feeling of a town and a tower block of flats or offices would represent a city. An industrial scene can easily be created by incorporating cooling towers or large factories in the picture. The possibilities for railway photography in urban and industrial setting are very great and should provide a challenge to the ingenuity of the photographer.

It is worth mentioning here that whether you are photographing in town or the country, home or abroad, if possible always have at hand good detailed maps. This will save time in helping you get to locations more easily.

By including tower blocks of flats in this setting for this shot of a Class 47 with a Leeds–York train we help to create the atmosphere of a city, in this case Leeds. The date is 11 November 1980.

Camera, Nikon FM with 85mm lens plus yellow filter. Exposure is 1/500th sec at f5·6. Film, Ilford FP4 (rated at 160ASA), developed in Aculux.

Cooling towers, factories, pylons and the M6 motorway all combine to produce an industrial setting for this picture of Brush Class Type 47 No 47341 on an eastbound train of hopper wagons. The location is Bromford Bridge, east of Birmingham on 14 April 1982.

Camera, Nikon FM with 50mm lens plus yellow filter. Exposure 1/500th sec at f5·6. film, Ilford FP4, rated at 200ASA and developed in Acuspecial.

Preserved LNER Pacific No 4472 *Flying Scotsman* crosses Broadsands viaduct on the Dart Valley Railway's Torbay line with an evening Paignton to Kingswear train on 22 July 1973. Notice how the viaduct, situated on the 1 in 60 climb towards Churston, is framed by the trees and how the train stands out clearly against the waters of Torbay. Low evening sun highlights the train and viaduct.

Camera Nikkormat with 50mm lens and yellow filter. Exposure 1/500th sec at f5·6. Film Ilford FP4 rated at 125ASA developed in I D11 (undiluted).

(c) Bridges and Viaducts

Many of us are fascinated by bridges and viaducts. The sight of the Forth bridge or Ribblehead viaduct often makes us think of man's tremendous battle against nature and the elements when they were constructed. Many of these magnificent structures are very photogenic in their own right and if you add the presence of a train you have a complete railway scene full of beauty and interest. But there is an art in photographing such structures and you cannot approach it in any old fashion and expect to get good results.

As with locomotives certain types of viaducts and bridges look better from some angles than others. With some river bridges for example you may decide to film from a low angle not only because it may be more photogenic but simply to conclude the riverside scene (boats etc) and if the water is calm enough, reflections of the train. But be careful when filming from lower angles as many bridges and viaducts have quite high parapets at the sides which will obviously obscure part of the train. One way round this is if there is a clear section at the end of the bridge or viaduct is to wait until the locomotive and part of the train has reached this and then take it; by so doing this you will only obscure the back part of the train. With viaducts, because they generally span valleys, it may be better to take a view from above, if possible, to include much of the surrounding hills and slopes in your picture.

These suggestions are meant as guide lines and a certain amount of experiment may be necessary before satisfactory results are achieved.

There will be certain physical problems when photographing many viaducts and bridges; the main one is when you are unable to get close enough to the subject in order to get a reasonably balanced picture. This can be overcome to a certain extent by the use of telephoto lenses. These lenses are ideal for taking scenes side-on but when filming from the three-quarter front position if you use extra long telephoto lenses you may find that the viaduct or bridge is too distorted by foreshortening for your taste.

There are also times when a wide angle lens is very useful, especially shooting a scene from a lower angle. By using this lens you are able to get close into the subject and still get a balanced picture.

(d) Tunnels and deep cuttings

Generally locations around tunnels and deep cuttings are not as well lit as more open spaces. Because of this it is important to allow more exposure in these type of locations. The only circumstances when this may not be the case is when a location is so geographically placed that at certain times of the day it may be in full sunlight. It is important to take care when photographing steam locomotives around tunnels because of the problems that can be caused by the exhaust. If you are too near the mouth of the tunnel and the exhaust is excessive the point of the picture will be lost. In most circumstances it is better to let the train get well clear of the tunnel mouth and then shoot it.

The problems of photographing steam trains around tunnels and cuttings are emphasised in this picture of GWR pannier tank No 5764 emerging from Knowlsands tunnel (Severn Valley Railway) on 10 August 1974, with a Bewdley–Bridgnorth train. Note the locomotive is well clear of the tunnel mouth thus avoiding problems with exhaust etc.

As is so often the case in this type of location lighting can present many exposure problems. This was particularly so in this case where the sunlight was coming from the side and back. To overcome this problem it was necessary to give more exposure to the shadow areas (front of locomotive etc) and burn in the highlights (side of the train and trees on left hand side) at the printing stage.

Camera, Nikkormat with 50mm lens plus yellow filter. Exposure 1/500th sec at f5·6. Film, Ilford FP4, rated at 200ASA and developed in Acuspecial.

(e) Signals

The inclusion of semaphore signals invariably adds interest to any railway photograph. Indeed there are many drab locations which have been transformed by this factor.

One way of enhancing any scene is to frame the train with signals, particularly if it is a large gantry. A good depth of field is obviously needed for success in these type of pictures so that signals and train are all well in focus. The use of a standard or wide angle lens (obviously plus good lighting conditions enabling you to use smaller lens apertures) should not only ensure this but is probably a necessity to include all of the signals and at the same time get a good balance on the train. If for physical reasons you do have to use a medium telephoto lens it is most important to use as small an aperture (high f number) as is possible, otherwise you will have too shallow a depth of field for satisfactory results. Also because of their rapid demise the photographing of semaphore signals in themselves is very important from an historical point of view, so it is always worth while taking them even if there is no train.

Colour-light signals, while not so attractive as semaphores, are very much part of today's railway scene and as such can be an integral part of any modern traction photograph. A low rear view of a train facing into a colour-light signal can be particularly effective in showing the signal aspect.

A very ordinary scene has been enhanced by the inclusion of semaphore signals. This, combined with good lighting and cloud effects, helps to make a satisfying composition. The location is Burton Salmon south of York on the Leeds line and the train is a northbound passenger hauled by Brush Class 47 No 47279, 24 May 1981.

Camera, Nikon FM with 50mm lens plus yellow filter. Exposure 1/1000th sec at f4·5. Film, Ilford FP4 rated at 160ASA and developed in Aculux.

This is an obvious example of framing a train with a semaphore signal gantry here situated at Scarborough. The scene shows A3 Pacific *Flying Scotsman* leaving the station with a special train for York, 26 August 1981.

Camera, Nikon FM with 50mm lens plus yellow filter. Exposure 1/250th sec at f5·6. Film, Ilford XP1 rated at 400ASA and developed in XP1 chemicals.

(f) Stations

Most stations have an atmosphere all of their own, whether it be a little country station with cosy flower beds or a busy main line station like York with its wonderful roof and architecture and bustling crowds. Atmosphere is the key word in a station photograph and somehow we have to convey this aspect.

There are three basic ingredients in stations scenes — architecture, trains and human activity. The first two together will nearly always make satisfactory pictures providing that you get a balance between the train and architecture and that one does not cancel out the other. For example if you are photographing at say an ex GWR station if you let the train obscure too much of the scene the picture will lose its identity and could in fact have been taken anywhere.

Human activity is all important in station scenes and in fact many fine pictures have been taken of this alone. This is particularly so in big stations where people are involved in many different types of jobs that are all part of the railway scene and naturally passengers are also a vital ingredient of any station scene.

Add human activity to the first two ingredients — architecture and trains — and this combination should give you scope for many fine pictures. Concerning exposure, problems only really arise when photographing in covered stations and great care must be taken to avoid under exposure.

With regard to what lenses to use for station scenes this entirely depends on the location but I would regard a combination of standard, short telephoto and medium wide angle lenses as sufficient for all types of pictures; indeed a standard lens alone would get you by in most situations.

A pair of Class 5 4–6–0s Nos 44477 and 45352 trundle through Snow Hill station on the evening of 12 August 1966. This picture illustrates a city station with its large number of tracks and spacious platforms, colour-light signals, over all roof and canopies. In the distance, crowds can be seen waiting for arrivals and a period spotter is on the left hand side of the picture. The whole scene is overlooked by a typical city centre office block.

Camera, Konica 35mm range-finder with 45mm lens plus yellow filter. Exposure 1/250th sec at f4. Film, Kodak Plus X (125ASA), developed in D 76 (undiluted).

(g) Sheds or depots

This type of photography can be divided into two distinct types:

(1) Pictures taken inside the shed, usually of locomotives at rest.

(2) Activities in the shed yard, watering, coaling, refuelling, maintenance, being turned etc.

For success in the first type of picture, because you will probably be working in a reasonably confined space it would be better to use a standard or medium wide angle lens and in some cases, because there is insufficient light, it may be necessary to use a tripod. If you do not have a tripod handy try wedging yourself against a wall or post and this may help to steady your shot. I should add that since in this case you will be on railway property and will need a permit to be there you should check that tripods will not cause a hazard to staff safety.

As with all indoor photography exposure can be a problem and it may well be worth while taking several shots of the same scene at different exposures.

Outdoor shed activity can provide plenty of scope and there are many opportunities to create atmospheric and evocative pictures. If available a wide variety of lenses could be used to good advantage and experiment should be the order of the day.

As with station photography human activity can play an important part of shed photography and should not be overlooked.

A sunny summer afternoon at St Austell station, Cornwall as *Western Sovereign* pulls through with an up parcels train passing another Western type diesel in an up loop with an empty stock train, 8 August 1968. St Austell is a typical example of an ex GWR country station with its splendid footbridge, station buildings and semaphore signals. Flower beds and surrounding trees complete the scene.

Camera, Konica range-finder with 45mm lens plus yellow filter. Exposure 1/500th sec at f6·3. Film, Kodak Plus X (125ASA), developed in D76 (undiluted).

(h) From the footplate and train

If you are lucky enough to get a rarely granted permit to ride on the footplate or cab of a locomotive it is certainly worthwhile attempting to take photographs. The most popular type of picture from this position is surely the view from the cab window. To get good results in these circumstances it would be better to use a standard lens which will give you a good depth of field and fairly fast shutter speed to avoid camera shake which is an obvious problem in a vibrating locomotive cab.

Another type of shot is to show the men at work in the cab. Because of the confined space you will probably obtain better results by using a medium wide angle lens.

Before taking any footplate picture try to adopt a firm stance, if possible by wedging your body against something solid. This again will help to cut down on camera shake.

On some steam locomotives you will find a cab that is all 'bulled up'. This can make a very attractive subject, especially in colour (see colour picture on page 39.) For this type of picture you obviously take it when the locomotive is stationary and again you may find that a wide angle lens is very useful for this type of shot.

Photographing the locomotive from the carriage window of the train can also be very rewarding. Once again a firm stance and fast

Croes Newydd shed (Wrexham) on the afternoon of 13 March 1967 is the setting for this portrait of standard Class 4 4–6–0 No 75002.

Good lighting from the shed entrance (on the left) and sunlight from the roof combine to create beautiful patterns of light on the locomotive and surroundings. Note the shadow of the chimney on the adjoining tender.

Great care was taken with the exposure for this picture, allowing plenty of exposure for the shadow areas (essential in this type of shot) and the highlights were burnt in at the printing stage. Notice also how the locomotive is framed by the foreground and roof.

Camera, Konica range-finder with 45mm lens. Exposure 1/60th sec at f4. Film, Kodak Plus X (125ASA), developed in D 76 (undiluted).

There is plenty of human (and animal) activity in this picture of a Polish class PX48 narrow gauge 0–8–0 No 1736 at Krosnewice shed, southern Poland, 5 September 1975. It is interesting to note the method of coaling the locomotive.

Camera, Nikkormat with 50mm lens plus yellow filter. Exposure 1/250th sec at f5·6. Film Ilford FP4 (rated at 200ASA), developed in Acuspecial.

View from a carriage window. The train was a special working from Regua to Chaves on the Portuguese metre gauge, hauled by Henschel 2–4–6–0 tank locomotive No E214, 3 June 1969.

The tight curves usually found on narrow gauge lines offer ample opportunity for this type of shot. The symmetry of the reflection is given extra interest by the carriage window frame being slightly off centre. Obviously a firm stance and grip is most important for this type of shot, meaning of course as fast a shutter speed as is possible.

Camera, Konica range-finder with 45mm lens plus yellow filter. Exposure 1/500th sec at f5·6. Film, Kodak Plus X (125ASA), developed in D 76 (undiluted).

shutter speed are pre-requisites for satisfactory pictures. It is better to position yourself some way from the locomotive, around the middle to the back of the train (depending on the length of the train) and shoot when the train is on a tight curve. If you are a long way from the front of the train a medium telephoto lens might be the ideal lens to use but if you are not too far away a standard lens should suffice.

From this position it is also possible to photograph oncoming trains on an adjoining track. Resist the temptation. It is highly dangerous.

Always have your camera handy when a train stops at a station because very often there will be a station scene or locomotive in front of your eyes that is worth photographing and you have only a split second to get your picture. A standard or wide angle lens should be the best lens for the job and it is in these circumstances that an automatic camera comes into its own.

View from a cab window, in this case South African Railways class GMA Garratt locomotive No 4064 as it trundles through Capitol Park shed yard, Pretoria. A shutter speed of 1/500th sec was necessary to avoid camera shake and standard lens at an aperture of f4 has given a reasonable depth of field. The date 20 July 1981.

Camera, Nikon FM 50mm lens plus yellow filter. Film, Ilford Pan F (50ASA), developed in I D11 (undiluted).

(i) Panning and pacing

Panning is a way of creating the illusion of speed by catching a sharp image of the locomotive against a blurred background. The technique relies on swinging the camera round (with the direction in which the train is travelling) to match the speed of the locomotive as it passes while using a shutter speed that is slow enough to show the rest of the scene as a blur. By using too fast a shutter speed, say a 1/500th or 1/1000th sec you will not only get a sharp engine but everything else will probably be sharp, which will ruin the pan effect.

How slow a shutter speed to choose depends primarily on the speed of the locomotive. If the locomotive is on an express moving fairly fast along a long straight then a shutter speed of 1/125th sec should be suitable. However if your train is doing around 25mph on a preserved line something around a 1/30th sec should answer your needs. But remember when using shutter speeds below a 1/125th sec it is advisable to use a tripod to avoid camera shake. As the shutter speed you will be using will be slow, in most lighting conditions, the aperture of the lens will therefore be small (high f number). Because of this factor it is better to use a medium speed film when panning (around 100ASA) for if you use too fast a film you may find that you would sometimes need a smaller aperture than your lens possesses. At this point it is also worth remembering that in poor lighting conditions when you only have a medium or slow speed film in your camera that panning is one way to get a good sharp picture of the locomotive which would otherwise be a blur.

Your choice of lens depends on your location. As the ideal place to

This picture was taken on the footplate of 0–6–0 saddle tank *Empress* at Cadley Hill colliery (near Burton-on-Trent) on 23 November 1972. Note the shallow depth of field due to the use of a wide lens aperture which in turn has focused attention on the driver. Also note the diagonal line from the driver's hand through to the yoke of his jacket which adds energy to the picture.

Camera, Nikkormat with 50mm lens. Exposure 1/500th sec at f2·8. Film, Ilford FP4 (125ASA), developed in I D11 (undiluted).

Class V2 2–6–2 No 4771 *Green Arrow* at speed south of York with a York circular train, 25 June 1978. As the train was moving at around 50–60 mph I was able to use a shutter speed of 1/125th sec and still get a blurred background. Also a lens aperture of f8 ensured a good depth of field, thus avoiding any focusing problems.

Camera, Nikkormat with 50mm lens plus yellow filter. Exposure 1/125th sec at f8. Film, Ilford FP4 rated at 160ASA and developed in Aculux.

catch your engine is broadside on to you, you will need plenty of space along the line to give you room to stand back. These spaces are to be found on multi-track lines and places such as demolished stations, or in open fields where the track is raised clear of the fence. It follows that if you are in a confined space a standard to medium wide angle lens is better and if you are some distance away you may need a short telephoto lens. However before choosing your lens it is important to find out the size of the locomotive as a small tank engine takes up a fraction of a large tender engine or a diesel express locomotive. You must choose a location and lens that will let you capture the whole of the locomotive plus part of the leading carriage or wagon and perhaps a third again to allow for misjudgement.

Focusing should not be too much of a problem because you know exactly where the locomotive is going to be and therefore can pre-determine your focus setting. Also because on most occasions you will be using smaller lens apertures (around f8 — f16) this will give you far greater depth of focus. However

remember that this depth of focus is greater on standard and wide angle lenses than on telephotos.

The technique of panning is to swing the camera round to match the speed of train, firing the shutter when the locomotive is directly opposite to you and framed in the camera, but still carrying on swinging the camera during and after the shutter has been fired until the train is away from you.

The most common mistake is in 'targeting' the subject, instead of firing the shutter when the locomotive is fully side on to you and across to the edge of the frame. In the excitement the shutter is fired when the camera is centred on the front of the locomotive thus spoiling the pan. Practice first with a few dummy runs on cars passing nearby.

Another mistake is in not matching the swing of the camera to the speed of the locomotive. This can take several forms, from weaving the lens up and down to jerking to a halt when pressing the button. Practice makes perfect. Like a golfer you must follow the swing through smoothly after making contact. This is when a tripod (used

Class 5 4–6–0 No 4767 nears Hexham with a train from Newcastle, 6 June 1981.

This is a panned shot that has obviously been taken too soon. The position is wrong, I should have stood more to the left to allow the locomotive to clear the obscuring bush in the right foreground and the telegraph pole.

Also as the train was travelling at around 25–30 mph the shutter speed that I used (1/125th sec) was too fast and in this case a shutter speed of a 1/60th sec or even less was needed to blur the background and the wheels of the locomotive still further.

Camera, Nikon FM with 50mm lens plus yellow filter. Exposure 1/125th sec at f8. Film, Ilford FP4, rated at 160ASA and developed in Aculux.

with a loose head) can be very useful especially when you are using telephoto lenses which are generally heavier than standard or wide angle lenses.

You will get a more pronounced movement or blurring from objects which are close to you and have a soft shape. The ideal location is a line running in front of a bank of trees or bushes. The sky is not much use as a background as it has so little texture that the blurred effect would be lost. Sharply defined shapes such as telephone poles are a problem as they spoil the horizontal streaks which create the flow of movement, and it is also difficult to judge the precise moment to photograph the train, without finding a pole sticking up through the chimney.

Pacing the train is panning from a vehicle which is moving at the same speed as the train. The main example would be from a car being driven on a long straight road without junctions, parallel to the track. The same conditions apply here as with panning from a standing position but because you are moving at the same speed as the train there is no need to swing the camera round with the train. Simply frame the subject and fire the shutter when it is side on to you. Obviously you need a second person with you to drive the car, a clear road and the train moving at low to medium speed. Under no circumstances should you attempt to drive and film at the same time, nor should it be attempted if other traffic is in the road since in the stress of the moment an accident can so easily be caused, and certainly it should not be attempted with a train travelling at express speeds.

In a car your main difficulty will be judging the best moment between telegraph poles and trees, as you cannot look ahead, only sideways. Your drivers must warn you of such things as lineside features blocking the view, and the rise and fall of the road relative to the line. Be prepared to use a roll of film in order to get two or three decent shots because you need a considerable amount of luck to achieve a reasonable pacing shot.

One further point regarding shutter speeds, because you obviously cannot use a tripod inside a car and with the movement of the car itself, it would be better to use a shutter speed of 1/125th sec, certainly no slower, and possibly 1/250th sec.

Panning and pacing are used deliberately to create the image of speed or possibly to salvage a good picture when the light is failing. They can also be used to good advantage when a sideways view is the only reasonable one, such as when a steam locomotive is travelling tender first. Another use for panning could be when the landscape is not very photogenic and reducing it to a blur makes up for its deficiencies.

This technique can also be very useful when photographing modern traction, the impression of speed given in a good pan shot can make up for the lack of exhaust.

(j) Railway Architecture
Stations in particular are worth photographing for their own sakes, whether or not a train is standing on a platform. The old stations, richly decorated in the great metropolis, or ornamented with simple rustic charm in the country, are all worth recording, before they are modernised or closed. There are still treasures to be unearthed even on lines that have been abandoned. If nobody makes a record of them now, who will know what they looked like in a hundred years' time?

Before the separate rail companies were nationalised under the name of British Railways, each company proudly stamped its signature with initials cast into the frames of seats and in roof brackets. The style of semaphore signals, whether upper or lower quadrants, and the design of signalboxes, were unique to the company that ran the line. Each company had its livery and colour scheme for the paintwork, such as light and dark stone on the Great Western, and each set of colours denoted the company's influence as surely as the capital letters woven into the design of the metal castings. Whenever a preserved line is borrowed for a film sequence, the experienced eye will derive great pleasure from checking that the details are consistent.

Modern stations, although not so rich in detail, also have some photogenic features. The use of large areas of plate glass enables the photographer to see more different activities at the same time. Although familiarity dulls the powers of observation, we should try to record for posterity the most characteristic scenes of a period or event, such as the advertisements, the blackboard carrying notice of changes, the kind of people who use the services and the way they are dressed. Mini-skirts in profusion for example would date photographs to the late 1960s. Many photographs are brought to life when they include some human activity, and all these little details go to make your photographs something special. Once again a standard or medium wide angle lens would seem to be ideal for these type of pictures.

Filmed from the car is South African Railways Class 25NC 4–8–4 No 3525 at speed with a northbound goods on the famous De Aar–Kimberley line. The location is Houtkraal and the date 30 July 1982.

Camera, Super Ikonta 6 x 6cm with 75mm lens. Exposure 1/125th sec at f6·3. Film, Ilford FP4 (rated at 125ASA), developed in I D11 (undiluted).

A Birmingham–Kidderminster DMU enters Hagley station on 28 October 1981. This GWR footbridge is a fine example of railway architecture; notice the circular decorations bearing the initials GWR and date of construction 1884.

Camera, Super Ikonta 6 x 6cm with 75mm lens. Exposure 1/250th sec at f4. Film, Ilford FP4 (rated at 125ASA), developed in I D11 (undiluted).

East German narrow gauge. A pair of Meyer 0–4–4–0 tank engines Nos 99 1561 and 99 1585 leave Wolkenstein with a freight consisting of standard gauge wagons on transporters for Johstad, 24 February 1981. Although, because of the misty conditions, the train appears as a semi-silhouette, the attractive setting compensates for the lack of detail. Note also how in these cold and damp conditions the exhausts of the locomotives cling in the air.

Camera, Nikon FM with 50mm lens plus yellow filter. Exposure 1/500th sec at f4. Film, Ilford FP4 (rated at 160ASA), developed in Aculux.

6

Weather and Lighting

Except when carried out in sheds, museums and some stations, railway photography is an outdoor pursuit and in consequence is open to all the elements and the problems that they can bring. In this chapter we shall deal with the different types of weather and lighting conditions that may be encountered and the technical problems that can arise from them.

Weather
(a) Fog and mist
Because of the general lack of light in foggy and misty conditions, to obtain reasonable results it is essential to use a fairly fast film, certainly no less than 125ASA and preferably around 400ASA. As a general rule in these sort of conditions it is better to fill the frame with the locomotive and train

rather than concentrating on landscape work. There are exceptions especially in attractive settings, for example when a train is crossing a river but in most cases like this the train will probably appear as a semi-silhouette.

One of the many problems encountered in foggy conditions is the lack of depth in the picture. This can be countered to a certain extent

by the use of a strong foreground such as a wall, hedge or clump of rocks etc. A certain amount of ingenuity is required to obtain good results in fog and mist and you will need to experiment.

Exposure is also a problem in these sorts of conditions (it tends to look brighter than it actually is) and great care must be taken to avoid errors, especially in the case of under exposure. If you are not careful you will finish up with such a thin negative that is almost impossible to print to a reasonable standard, and if you are using colour reversal film, a transparency that is too dark for any sort of projection.

But having said all this, pictures taken on misty days, especially of steam at work, have an atmosphere of their own and some very satisfying compositions can be obtained in these conditions.

The conditions when I took this picture were pretty appalling – torrential rain! However thanks to my wife who held the umbrella I was able to achieve a satisfying picture. The rain has added sparkle to the rails and sleepers, rooftops and bushes and has highlighted the locomotive and train, and the damp conditions have also meant good steam effects.

As the lighting conditions were dull (the exposure was a 1/250th sec at f3·5 using 400 ASA film) I used a medium wide angle lens to obtain greater depth of field.

The location is the entrance to Standedge tunnel on the Diggle route and the train is the SLOA Trans-Pennine Pullman hauled by Class 5 4–6–0 No 5305 on 26 September 1981.

Camera, Nikon FM with 35mm lens. Exposure 1/250th sec at f3·5. Film, Ilford XP1 (rated at 400ASA), developed in XP1 chemicals.

The disastrous effect of wind on steam locomotives is well illustrated in this picture of Nos 5000 and 80079 north of Church Stretton with a special train on 19 April 1980. As the sun and wind were coming from opposite sides nothing could really have been done about this except hope that the wind would drop for a few seconds enabling me to achieve a successful picture, but obviously this gamble did not pay off. In fact I took around a dozen pictures (using a motor drive) of this scene and every one to me was a disaster.

Camera, Nikon FM with 85mm lens plus yellow filter. Exposure 1/500th sec at f6·3. Film, Ilford FP4 (rated at 160ASA), developed in Aculux.

(b) Rain

Rain can certainly be a hazard to the railway photographer, especially in Britain, where we seem to have more than our fair share. But what can be a disadvantage can sometimes turn things to our advantage. This is especially so on a dull day when the advent of rain can add much sparkle to an otherwise drab scene. The metal of the rails glistens and locomotives and trains can take on a very shiny and photogenic appearance, and exhausts hang in the air. Puddles on the platforms bring opportunities for reflections. So do not give up because it is raining; you may be more than a little surprised with the results. But remember to take a good strong umbrella to keep yourself and your equipment dry. And if possible have someone with you who will hold the umbrella for you — wives and girl friends please note.

When it rains really hard, larger stations can usually provide a certain amount of cover from which to operate and so avoid getting very wet. This is worth bearing in mind when you want to photograph an important train and the weather bars you from the more open locations.

(c) Wind.

Wind is not a problem when photographing diesel and electric traction but is certainly a serious hazard as far as steam is concerned. Many fine steam shots have been spoiled because of strong wind causing the exhaust to blow over the side of the engine and covering the engine in 'clag'. This is especially so if the wind and sun are coming from the opposite directions. The most practical thing to do in these circumstances is to take the picture from as low an angle as possible (if practical from below rail level) and by doing this, with a bit of luck you may get a decent picture with the exhaust just clear of the train, but this is not always the case and you may have many failures. The other alternative is to take the picture against the light — in other words create a silhouette and this will be discussed later on in this chapter.

Of course if the sun is not out you can take your picture from the windward side, which will effectively cut out any problems. But 'Murphy's Law' being what it is, with strong winds you inevitably get sunshine from the opposite side, and even blustery winds can momentarily change direction and cause the exhaust from a steam special to swirl.

(d) Snow

During the winter of 1981/2 much of Britain was gripped by very severe weather with temperatures as low as minus 20°C and thick snow. In some parts it was like that for more than a week and on the days when it was not snowing there was a lot of sunshine. This type of weather can be a bonus to the railway photographer because railway snow scenes, particularly when you add sunshine, can be among the most beautiful and atmospheric pictures that it is possible to obtain — always assuming the weather does not stop the trains, or your ability to reach a suitable location.

The greatest problem that snow brings is the one of assessing the correct exposure. When photographing in the snow take a meter reading for the snow area and one for the main subject — if it is not static but an action shot, estimate exposure for the train (remembering that the train will be much darker than snow and will require far more exposure). Then effect a compromise on the different meter readings. If there is a wide difference, always err on the side of the main subject. For example if you have a 400ASA film in the camera, meter readings might be as follows:-

Snow area – 1/500th sec at f8 – f11
Train – 1/500th sec at f5·6

Set the lens to an aperture of f6·3 (still at 1/500th sec for the shutter) which exposure should give you plenty of detail in the main subject and not too much over exposure in the snow areas. But a word of warning. It is alright to have a certain amount of over exposure when using negative film in these weather conditions but when you are using colour reversal film in adverse conditions like snow, it is probably better to stick to the general meter reading, which will give you a slightly darker and perhaps more dramatic slide but more important will retain more detail in the highlights. Moreover with sun on snow, the darker parts of the train will be bottom lit with light reflected off the snow.

Sunshine and snow invariably form the basis for attractive railway photographs as can been see in this shot of a Longbridge bound DMU as it approached the University station in the suburbs of Birmingham, 8 December 1981. The canal on the right hand side is the Worcester-Birmingham canal.

With regard to the exposure for this picture, I took a reading for the snow area which was around f11 at 1/500th and a reading for the surrounding bushes which was f5·6 at 1/500th. I assumed that the reading for the bushes would be similar to that of the train. I then bracketed the two exposures and decided that an aperture of around f6·3 would give me a reasonably correct exposure, and highlights were burnt in at the printing stage.

Camera, Nikon FM with 50mm lens yellow filter. Exposure 1/500th sec at f6.3. Film, Ilford XP1 (rated at 400ASA), developed in XP1 chemicals.

When blizzard conditions prevail you really need a dark background to emphasise the driving snow. One idea would be to photograph a train as it emerges from under a bridge. If you set the train against the sky you will tend to lose the effect of the falling snow.

When out in these sort of conditions always wrap up warmly and take an umbrella as protection for you and your equipment. While dealing with the protection of equipment in extremely cold weather to avoid things like shutter and battery failure, etc, keep your camera as warm as possible either in a camera gadget bag or case or even inside your jacket.

On days when it is actually snowing, the lighting factors are similar to those in fog and mist. The engine appears as a semi-silhouette, and the landscape recedes into paler shades of grey. But where snow lies on the ground it gives extra lightness to otherwise sombre areas, and of course where it clings to branches, fences etc it brings a sparkling dimension of textures to the picture, as shown in the previous picture. But these bushes and sheds were still dark and served to show up the driving snowflakes, increasing the wintry feel-

ing. The use of a fast film with its conspicuous grain adds to this effect. Notice how the angles of the exhaust and the rough verges lead the eye to the locomotive, helped by the man walking up to it.

The setting for this industrial scene is West Cannock Colliery, Staffs, on 19 December 1969 and the locomotive is *Topham*, a Bagnall 0–6–0 saddle tank.

Camera, Konica range-finder with 45mm lens. Exposure 1/250th sec at f4. Film, Kodak Tri-X (rated at 400ASA), developed in D 76 (undiluted).

This picture of Western class diesel No D1048 *Western Lady* with a Birmingham–Paddington train near Harbury on 17 April 1976 is a good example of even lighting with no really dense shadow to present exposure problems. The light reading used was that taken for the whole scene without any adjustment.

Camera, Nikkormat, 50mm lens plus yellow filter. Exposure 1/500th sec at f5·6. Film, Ilford FP4 (rated at 160ASA), developed in Aculux.

Lighting

In the chapter on equipment we discussed the lens aperture or iris which controls the amount of light that enters the camera, the size of the opening being indicated by the f number. The lower the f number, ie f1·8 the more light is allowed in, and the higher the f number, f16, the less light is allowed in. So when we talk about over exposing by one stop on a meter reading we mean using a lower f number and the opposite in the case of under exposure. For example:-

    Meter reading = 1/250th sec at f8

    One stop over exposure = 1/250th sec at f5·6

    One stop under exposure = 1/250th sec at f11

The same effect can be obtained by adjusting the camera shutter speed and keeping the aperture static at f8. To over expose by one stop you would use the next slower shutter speed (1/125th sec) and to under expose by one stop the next highest (1/500th sec). If you wish to over or under expose by two stops you must alter the shutter speed either down or up by two speeds and so on. This last method may be more useful on occasions, certainly when taking stills to allow a higher aperture f number to be used which gives greater focal length.

(a) Normal lighting

By normal lighting we simply mean even lighting, and this comes in two major categories. The first is when there is no clear sunlight and virtually everywhere has an evenness of light about it from continuous cloud cover. The second category is when there is bright sunlight and you are taking the photograph with the sun behind you. The whole scene is more or less evenly illuminated by the sun, without the dense shadows and extreme contrast provided by side lighting.

In both of these situations exposure should not present a problem and straightforward meter readings of the main scene will probably suffice for reasonably accurate exposures resulting in good negatives and transparencies. The only thing to be careful of is when photographing a dark or black locomotive particularly in colour. In these circumstances it would to prudent to over expose slightly and open up the lens by a half to one stop (use a lower f number) to obtain maximum detail in the main subject – the locomotive.

There are occasions when although you have the sunlight on the front of the subject you are physically unable to take the photograph from the sunny side and in consequence the side of the subject is in shadow. Providing that the shadow area is not too dense it is still possible to get a satisfactory picture by allowing extra exposure for the shadow area. This is especially so if you are using black and white film but does not always work out as well with colour film because of the obvious loss of colour in the subject (shadow) area.

(b) Side and back lighting.

Side lighting is given when you take a photograph with the sun roughly at right angles to the line of vision of your camera, creating strong highlights and shadows. Back lighting is provided when that angle is even more extreme, perhaps only illuminating the details of the edges of the subject (see lower picture on page 16). This type of lighting can be used to best advantage when the sun is low in the sky, especially early in the morning and late in the afternoon. The effect of side and back lighting is to throw the subject into strong relief. This is very apparent when photographing hard edged metalic subject like locomotives and trains.

The use of a lens hood is a must when photographing in this type of lighting to avoid any flare on the lens, and it is important to position the camera so that sun is not actually shining into the lens.

Obviously when the sun is low the shadows are longer and can form a dramatic part of the composition. But this in turn creates some exposure problems. It is very important to retain a certain amount of detail in the shadow area, otherwise you will finish up with shadows that are far too dense and contrasty.

This is very pronounced in monochrome work, the results being known in the trade as 'soot and whitewash' prints. So great care must be taken with exposure. Try working on an exposure that is a balance between the light reading for the shadow area and for the highlights.

This applies equally well when working with colour negative film but when using transparency film in these types of lighting conditions it is best to avoid too much over exposure because you may finish up with washed-out highlights. It is far better on a slide to have slightly denser and perhaps more dramatic shadows but retain good detail in the highlights.

Overleaf: In this picture the sun was on the front of the locomotive but of necessity was coming from the opposite side to the camera and so the side of the train was in shadow. I allowed extra exposure for this when filming and at the printing stage held back the shadow area to retain more detail.

The train is the 11.43 York to Kings Cross hauled by Deltic No 55016 *Gordon Highlander* and the location is Selby swing bridge on 24 May 1981.

Camera, Nikon FM with 85mm lens plus yellow filter. Exposure 1/500th sec at f4·5. Film, Ilford FP4 (rated at 160ASA), developed in Aculux.

(c) Silhouette

Basically a silhouette effect is created when you shoot the locomotive or train (or any other principal subject of the picture) totally against the light, so what you create is a black or very dark profile set against a light background, preferably like a dappled sky or rippling water for maximum effect. And these types of photographs certainly have impact and are equally effective when using either colour or black and white film.

The technique required for this type of picture is not at all difficult because all you really do is simply place the subject between the camera and light source. Take a meter reading for the background (that is, the light source) and expose for this. It should completely under

The lighting in this picture is opposite to the previous picture. The front of the locomotive is in shadow with full sunlight on the side of the train. But as in the previous picture extra exposure was given for the shadow area. At the printing stage the shadow area was held back and the highlights were burnt in. The scene shows 0–6–0 diesel shunter No 08068 at work at Bromford Bridge sidings, Birmingham, on 14 April 1982

Camera, Nikon FM with 135mm lens plus yellow filter. Exposure 1/500th sec at f6·3. Film, Ilford XP1 (rated at 400ASA) developed in XP1 chemicals.

expose the foreground and main subject, rendering them with very little detail (if in fact any at all) on the negative or transparency and in consequence creating the desired silhouette effect.

The maximum impact can be obtained when you have a low evening or morning sun. If you film against the light when the sun is high, even in silhouette work, be careful to shield the lens from the rays of the sun or you will finish up with far too much flare which will tend to spoil the overall effect.

You can often obtain a tremendous silhouette effect when filming a train crossing a bridge, particularly if it is the lattice girder type. Film from as low an angle as possible to create maximum effect.

Look out for the silhouette shot. You may be in a very ordinary location but by simply changing your position and shooting against the light you may well create a 'master shot'.

Silhouette at Waterside in south west Scotland as Barclay 0–4–0 saddle tank No 21 shunts on a tip near Dunaskin colliery, 30 August 1973. In this picture by using the exposure given by the light meter for the sky, I deliberately underexposed for the engine, rendering it as an almost black shape. This gave me the chance to show off the dramatic exhaust and cloud formations. Also, by choosing a low viewpoint, I could hide any intruding trees which might detract from this simple composition. The foreground is relieved by the shiny facets of coal, which would otherwise be too heavy and black.

Camera, Nikkormat with 35mm lens plus yellow filter. Exposure 1/500th sec at f8. Film, Ilford FP4 (rated at 200ASA), developed in Acuspecial.

7
Night Photography

An important aspect of railway photography and one that is so often neglected by the enthusiast is photographing the railway scene at night. The night time has much to offer the cameraman especially at a large station which looks entirely different when lit up from within. This also applies to locomotive depots where the juxtaposition of locomotives can create many unusual contrasts. And of course the steam locomotive at night can take on a dragon-like glow. Firelight fills the cab and picks out the faces of the crew. Sparks fountain up the chimney. Coals flicker with blue flames as the ashbox is raked out.

It is important to bear in mind that rail traffic is different at night. At the large stations mail and newspaper trains are either being loaded or unloaded (giving ample time for time exposures) and platforms are usually quite barren of passengers. At this point it seems prudent to mention that you should have either a platform or travel ticket. If a platform ticket is not required (as is the case at some open stations) because of security let someone in authority know of your presence and what you plan to do. With regard to locomotive depots you will require written permission before visiting them. An important safety factor is that you should wear something white or reflective and carry a pocket torch, which will be very useful for changing films, timing exposures, and checking apertures etc.

There are two main types of night photography, flashlight photography and taking pictures by available light (usually known as time exposures).

Flashlight

Flash guns are generally used for night shots, such as when a special train has returned and is waiting for its passengers to alight before the locomotive goes to shed. The locomotive is usually surrounded by enthusiasts, but if you are patient you can sometimes find a few seconds when the crowd pulls back and gives you a clear view of the engine. It is better to photograph from behind the crowd, looking at the backs of their heads, because otherwise their faces show up in flashlight as very pale patches which might upset the balance of your composition. In any case, nobody enjoys having a flash gun dazzling his eyes, especially the driver. You must not, incidentally, fire off a flash unit towards the cab of a moving train as this could temporarily blind the driver, which could have dangerous consequences.

Another situation where flashlight photography is useful is where a locomotive is standing on a track surrounded by poles and wires etc. In daylight, these would present such a cluttered appearance that your shot of the engine would be unacceptable. But at night, all these unwanted features would be lost in the darkness, while the locomotive would show up clearly silhouetted, pale against the black. Here, flash is better than an available light picture, where the poles might appear in your shot.

Some people use flash in daylight conditions which are very dull or gloomy, such as under station canopies. In these circumstances, the flash gun helps to fill in very heavy shadows. It also makes painted surfaces seem to be more glossy and adds sparkle to the fittings. This is because the source of light is a comparatively small point, unlike the sky, and any curved shiny surfaces will reflect this as more definite lines and points of light. This makes the locomotive stand out more brightly in its setting.

Most cameras are fitted with a hot-shoe into which your flash unit will fit. In this position, by means of a contact on the hot-shoe, the flash unit will fire simultaneously when the camera shutter is fired. Most cameras (with the exception of those which have leaf shutters fitted into their lenses) will have a shutter speed recommended for flash work, which you must use. If you set a faster speed you will end up with part of each frame blanked out.

It is possible to fire the flash gun independently of the hot-shoe. The camera may have a way of extending the circuit, synchronising the flash by a lead which plugs into the front of the camera. You can fire the camera with one hand and hold the flash with another. The advantage of this system is that you can separate the direction of the light from the angle of the camera's view. The light, coming from a different angle, will cast shadows on the subject, which the camera will be able to see, but would not do so if the flash was mounted on top of the camera. The shadows help to show up the shape of the locomotive in relief, which could make an interesting picture.

Your flash equipment, whether bulb or electronic, should have instructions for use, telling you how many times you can use the bulbs or roughly how many exposures your batteries will give you in your electronic flash. It is important when

Night study of former Somerset & Dorset 2-8-0 No 13809 at York on 24 October 1981 after working in with a special train. Because of the number of people around the locomotive this was a case where it would have been impossible to have used a time exposure. I settled for a portrait of the front end of the locomotive partly because of the people but also because of the very dark available lighting conditions (the locomotive was at the end of the platform and away from all the main station lighting). The use of a medium wide angle lens enabled me to move in fairly close to the subject, an obvious advantage with flash photography, and gave greater depth of field. The flash was held to the right of the camera and gives just a suggestion of shadow to such details as headlamp and buffers.

Camera, Nikon FM, lens 35mm. Electronic flash was used with an exposure setting of 1/125th sec (flash setting on Nikon FM) at f4. Film, XP1 (400ASA), developed in XP1 chemicals.

using electronic flash to have some idea of the re-cycling time required between each flash shot.

Most flash units are fitted with calculators (some are computerised) so that you can determine which aperture (f stop) to use. This is calculated by the speed of the film and the distance from the subject. For example if you are using a film with a speed of 50ASA and you are 20 to 30ft away from your subject this should enable you to use an aperture of around f3·5 and obtain a reasonable exposure. Simple flash calculators made of card can be obtained from photographic shops. Sometimes these simple card calculators are given away with photographic magazines.

Nevertheless, calculators are for use primarily indoors where the light source is fairly constant. But outdoors it is a different matter. A black-fronted steam locomotive will require more exposure than a yellow-fronted diesel. Thus in practice although exposures are determined by calculators you will need to experiment and make a careful note of your exposures to see what gives you the best results. Your first attempts will tell you a lot and you will develop an instinct for the possible.

When you buy an electronic flash unit primarily for use in railway photography, it is more important to buy a unit that will give you as much depth of light as possible, rather than one which has all the latest gadgets (important as these may be). But if you can afford a flash unit that has everything, this is even better.

Available light
When a locomotive or train is stationary you can take a picture using available light. By keeping the shutter of your camera open for a long time, even minutes, you should be able to achieve a satisfactory negative or transparency. These are known as time exposures. Most cameras have the symbol B at the slow end of the shutter speed scale. This letter B stands for bulb,

(originally shutters were operated by squeezing from a bulb) and on this setting the shutter will stay open as long as the shutter button is pressed in. To avoid any movement of the camera during the exposure you will need to mount the camera on a firm tripod and depress the shutter by a cable release that will lock in the depressed position. If you do not have a tripod and cable release and there is enough light to take your shot within the timed shutter settings (some of today's cameras have very slow shutter speeds) you can avoid camera shake by lodging the camera securely on a firm surface and winding back the 10 second delay lever (self timer) and then firing the shutter at the required speed. This means that the shutter will be fired independently after 10 seconds thus cutting out shake caused by the finger depressing the shutter button. This can work out well in an emergency but it is better to use a tripod and cable release if possible. Of course, if your camera is not fitted with a self timer, you will be unable to do this.

Wind can be another hazard. Try to find something to act as a windbreak to prevent your camera being vibrated or worse still blown over. On rough ground try to bed the legs of the tripod into the earth and stamp the soil firm.

When it is raining you will need to shelter your camera with, if possible, an umbrella. Check the lens before each exposure for drops of water on the surface and wipe dry with an old clean cotton handkerchief that will not leave any fluff on the glass. On foggy nights and in the small hours you may find condensation a problem, but frequent cleaning with the cloth should help.

Your next challenge will be judging the length of exposure to make. As every station and depot will have a different light intensity, inspired guesswork and experiment should help to solve the problem. If possible it is better to take two or three shots of the same subjects at various exposures, called bracketing the exposures. If you keep the lens aperture at around f8 to f16

(depending on the length of your lens, the longer the lens the higher the f number) and focus on a point say 30ft from your camera, then from around 15ft to infinity should be in focus. In other words you keep on a fixed aperture and vary your shutter speeds

eg 20 sec at f11
40 sec at f11
60 sec at f11

Time exposures at night really are guesswork but persevere (remembering to make a note of all exposures) and some quite startling results can be obtained.

Another useful idea when you are shooting time exposures is to 'paint in' the subject with a flash gun. You can use very long exposures on stationary subjects that are very poorly lit, leaving the camera's shutter open for a fair length of time and thus allowing you time to let off a flash gun near to the subject to paint it in. But you must be careful to hide yourself behind a corner when you let off the flash otherwise

This vignette of station architecture relies on a fairly small aperture and a longish 45 seconds time exposure to keep as much of the view in focus as possible. The only blurred shape is the driver of the DMU sorting through his paperwork. However because the general level of illumination was good and the direction of light was so similar to that of daylight, the photo loses the character of a night shot which is usually a subject well-lit from a low source against a dark background. On the plus side, the framing arch could only have been equally lit by artificial light.

On these low light readings, an ordinary meter is not reliable, because of 'reciprocity failure', ie the normal equivalents of shutter and aperture settings in the middle range of daylight do not hold true at the extreme ends of the scale. It is possible to use a specialist cadmium-sulphide meter for accurate low readings, but for general use, experience and 'bracketing the exposure' should suffice. The location was York on 30 August 1981.

Camera, Nikon FM with 35mm lens. Exposure 45 sec at f8. Film, XP1 (400ASA), developed in XP1 chemicals.

your image may be registered on the film. After firing the flash, if there is time, move on to another point of the subject and repeat the process.

As for the right lens to use for night photography, obviously telephoto lenses are out, but apart from using the standard lens it is well worth while considering using a wide angle lens. With a medium wide angle lens you are able to get closer to the subject, which is very useful when you are using flash. Also, because a wide angle gives a greater depth of field compared to a standard lens this may help with any focusing problems encountered in night photography. Railway photography at night is a challenge but one which can also be very rewarding and enjoyable.

Class 45 diesel locomotive No 45019 at York on the evening of 23 June 1981 with a southbound parcels train. Compared with the previous picture this is obviously a night-shot with low light sources and dark sky. Note the position of the station lights round the locomotive which add sparkle to the picture. The lighting has also brought out the shape of the cab and the similar curve of the main canopy.

Camera, Nikon FM with 35mm lens. Exposure 1¼ minutes at f8. Film, Ilford FP4 (rated at 160ASA), developed in Aculux.

8

Common Faults and Remedies

Fault. Picture out of focus. The background is sharp but the locomotive in the foreground blurred.

Remedy. Nothing can be done about a photograph that is out of focus, but if this happens to you, take very great care when focusing (as indeed you should always do) and if you still have this problem have your camera checked by a reliable repairer.

Fault. Too slow a shutter speed. The ballast and track under the locomotive is fairly sharp but the moving train train is blurred.

Remedy. Light permitting, always use a shutter speed which is fast enough to freeze the movement of the train. If lighting conditions do not permit this, if possible take the train more head on to slow the relative horizontal movement.

Fault. Camera shake. The whole of the picture is blurred through attempting to take a still shot, hand held, at far too slow a shutter speed (in this case an ⅛th of a second) which has caused camera shake.

Remedy. For this type of shot, where a slow shutter is required, always use a tripod and cable release. The only other way is to steady your body against something firm and hope that this will give a sharp picture.

Fault. Parapet of bridge included in shot. As many pictures are taken from these types of location this could be a recurring problem, especially if you use a range-finder camera where the picture in the viewfinder is slightly higher than the lens. Remember also that even with single lens reflex cameras the field of vision is not 100% of the picture that the camera is taking.

Remedy. Always take greater care to check that you have allowed enough clearance. One remedy is to raise your height by standing on something.

Fault. Objects protruding from top of locomotive and train.

Remedy. When filming in this type of location either film from a lower angle in order to let the train cover the background or film from a much higher angle (in this case the station foot bridge) in order to separate the train from the background, or provide a positive background.

Fault. Tender first locomotive too head on. Never take a tender or bunker first locomotive from this angle unless you want to finish up with a picture of a tender or bunker which is not really photogenic.

Remedy. For tender first pictures choose your location with great care to ensure as much of a side view of the locomotive and train as is possible unless you just want an 'operating' picture to show this type of working.

Fault. Subject taken too early, too far away and picture tilted.

Remedy. Obviously let the locomotive and train fill the frame without running out of it and look for the significant verticals/horizontals in order to align the picture correctly. The hill on the skyline provides a false horizontal here. Remember that telegraph poles and fence posts should be vertical but might not be. Buildings and structures ought to be.

Fault. Flash picture taken at wrong shutter speed for camera. Picture not upright.

Remedy. Always make sure the shutter of your camera is set on the correct speed setting for flash photography. These settings vary with different makes of camera, on some it is 1/80th sec, on others 1/125th of a sec and so on. Make sure camera is aligned.

Fault. Not winding on sufficient frames at beginning of film causing partial fogging of first frame (35mm only).

Remedy. This problem can be easily overcome by winding on an extra frame at the beginning of the film. Better to lose a frame than ruin a picture.

Fault. Photographers own shadow in picture. This problem can arise early morning or late evening and is easily overlooked by the photographer.

Remedy. Watch where you are standing. Alter the angle if possible. Shadow can be cut out at the printing stage (if using black and white or colour negative film) and colour transparencies can be masked but in both instances this may spoil the balance of the picture. Another solution would be (if possible) to use a longer lens and so cut out the shadows at source.

Fault. Cap left on camera lens.
    Remedy. !!!!

9
General Information

This section deals with the more general aspects of railway photography not covered in previous chapters but which are nevertheless very important not only in regard to railway photography but to photography in general.

Keeping records

This is an important but fairly simple thing to do but one which is often overlooked by the photographer. The best way I have found of keeping records is to note down each shot as you go along. I use two sets of notebooks, one for black and white and one for colour, and separate books for different subjects, ie British Railways (diesel and steam), overseas, industrial, etc. Each film is numbered BR 24, O 32, IND 14 etc.

As well as the obvious things to record like the date, locomotive number, location, etc, it is as well, particularly with black and white films to make a note of the film speeds, shutter speeds, apertures and conditions. These things can be useful later on, especially at the printing stage, allowing the best negatives to be selected. For example with negatives of similar pictorial content but taken at different shutter speeds and apertures (which can happen especially when chasing a train), a shot taken at a 500th at f6·3 will nearly always be sharper than one taken at a 250th at f4. This is not always apparent even when the negative is blown up in the enlarger (before the print is made) and it is sometimes only on the final print that any deficiencies become obvious. This information could save time and materials.

Below is an example of a record book layout.

Storing films and prints

(c) Negatives

After developing a roll of film, cut the film into strips of six for 35mm or strips of four for larger negative sizes, then store them in transparent negative sheets with the film number on the corner of the page. They can then be inserted into a loose leaf binder obtainable from most photographic shops labelled for the appropriate subject. As each sheet is numbered to correspond with the number in the record book it then becomes a simple matter to locate a particular negative. When the binders are full they will hold around 80 sheets of negatives.

(b) Transparencies

When I receive slides back from the processors I store them in slide boxes and keep a record in a master file (referring to my log book), numbering each transparency in date order. (See table below). Once I have done this I am free to take out the slides and put them into magazines which fit into slide projectors for use in slide shows but all the time I have a master record and it is an easy matter when I have finished with the slides to transfer them back to the slide boxes.

(c) Prints

Nowadays it is an easy matter to store prints. Albums of all sizes are

Fig 23 RECORD BOOK LAYOUT

FILM NO:		BR 112		FP4	125ASA		
Date	Place	Loco No	S/Sp	Ap	Conditions	Comments etc.	Neg No.
1/1/81	Bewdley SVR	43106	250	6.3	Bright	Light in stn.	1
10/1/81	Ais Gill	D47106	500	4	Dullish	S'bound pass	2
2/2/81	All Stretton	6201	500	5.6	Sun	S'bound Welsh Marches	3
2/2/81	S of Hereford	4930	500	4	Bright	S'bound Welsh Marches	4

Fig 24 TRANSPARENCY MASTER FILE

Date	Place	Loco No	Comments	Slide No
2/8/76	Lickey Bank	D45109	Sheffield train	1005
5/8/76	Carnforth	4472	On shed	1006
5/8/76	Carnforth	E86210	N'bound express	1007
6/8/76	Ravenglass	*River Irt*	Wtg to leave with Dalegarth tr.	1008

now made in which the print is slipped (face upwards) under a transparent sleeve, the back of the prints sticking to the page underneath. It is an easy matter to remove prints when required, for you just peel back the transparent cover and ease the print off the gummed page.

Care of equipment

(a) Cameras and lenses
Every two weeks or so it is as well to check all the shutter speeds on your cameras and also the delayed action lever. The slower shutter speeds may jam especially if, as is so often the case, they are very rarely used. The same applies to lenses; check all the apertures from the widest to the smallest opening.

Make it a rule to clean all equipment after use, especially lens surfaces. Also always carry a small brush to clean lenses while out on location. If your camera uses batteries, either for the meter or shutter or both, always carry spare batteries with you.

(b) Projectors and enlargers
What applies to cameras and lenses applies equally as well to projectors and enlargers. For the best results always keep the equipment clean, especially the lenses and condensors. Special anti-static lens cloths can be bought at most photographic stores. Also always check the motion on the enlarger column, making sure that it works smoothly. Last but not least always keep spare bulbs for the above equipment. Bulbs always have a nasty habit of going in the middle of a slide show or printing session.

(c) Flash equipment
Always make sure there is enough power for an evening's work by checking how long the unit takes to recharge after an exposure, and always carry spare batteries with you.

Points to remember
One of the most important things to remember with railway photography is that if you mess up a shot (and who has not?), it is extremely difficult to repeat that shot and in some cases impossible. With this in mind I have compiled the following list of do's and don'ts:

(1) Make sure your camera is always loaded with film. This is not as silly as it sounds and can happen to anyone amateur or professional alike. After all, to take a photograph, you have got to be in the right location, with a camera, and with that camera loaded.

(2) If your camera has a built-in meter be certain it is set to the correct film speed.

(3) Always wind on the film after taking the last exposure which in most cameras recocks the shutter automatically. It is an awful feeling to have the 'master shot' in your viewfinder only to press the shutter release and nothing happens because the shutter release lock has not been reset. Also make sure you have removed the lens cap.

(4) A point that comes up time and again in railway photography, simply because many pictures are taken from road bridges, is remembering to keep the camera clear of the parapet of the bridge. Many shots, particularly transparencies have been marred because of this. No camera viewfinder gives you 100% field of vision.

(5) Always use a lens hood. It may not always matter when taking a shot with the sun behind you but it is important when you turn quickly to take a three quarter rear shot and find yourself shooting against the sun. It also acts as some protection against rain and snow.

(6) If your camera uses batteries, always keep spare ones handy.

(7) Never get in the way of other photographers. This nearly always happens when people are chasing specials. Everyone is in position for their shot when just before the train arrives, up comes someone who runs into everyone's picture. People then shout at that person to move which in turn can cause obvious problems for people doing sound-ciné photography who by that time have very often started to film their sequence. Because of somebody's thoughtlessness many films are spoilt.

(8) Keep all unexposed films in a cool dry place and process as soon as possible after exposure.

(9) Finally, before taking your photograph adopt a firm stance, take a good deep breath and hold it until you have taken your shot. This will help to cut down on camera shake.

Submitting material for publications

(a) Colour
Processors of illustrations, whether for old-style letterpress blocks or modern film-based printing methods require colour transparencies from which to make the reproductions for colour photographs in books and magazines and *not* colour prints or negatives. Nor are copy transparancies normally accepted. In the past publishers have tended to prefer the larger size slide (6 x 6cm) but nowadays with the high standard of 35mm cameras and lenses and the modern high quality colour emulsions good quality 35mm transparencies are now quite acceptable provided they are clear, sharp and with good definition. Remember whatever size you send to the publisher always make sure that they have plenty of colour contrast and are correctly exposed.

Never send your slides mounted in glass (which can easily be broken in the post and so ruin your slides) but use card mounts, and write your name and subject matter clearly on the each mount submitted. As most slides are fairly precious it is as well to have copies made before sending them to publishers in case of loss.

(b) Black and white
For monochrome work a processor requires a black and white print and *not* a negative. The print *must* be on glossy paper, preferably glazed, and the best print size is either 16·5 x 21·6cm (8½in x 6½in) or 20·3 x 25·4cm (10in x 8in), no larger because of storage difficulties and ideally no smaller, even though the finished reproduction in the book may be smaller.

Like transparencies, make sure that prints are of good quality with plenty of contrasts. Prints tend to lose a little in processing for printing so it is important for the prints to contain strong blacks and whites and good sharp detail.

Make sure your name and subject matter is on the back of the every print, preferably on the edges and away from the clear areas of the print, ie the sky. Always write clearly but lightly so as to avoid print coming through to the emulsion side. With all material submitted give as much detail of the subject matter as is possible, for this will enable the editor to write a more detailed caption.

(c) General points
Always make sure that all material is well packed before posting. It is advisable to mark the packet PHOTOGRAPHIC MATERIAL PLEASE DO NOT BEND. Slides can be sent in the cartons that come with them from the processors. With regard to prints, insert a piece of card (a little larger than the prints) in the envelope with the photographs and this should suffice to keep the prints from being damaged. Publishers will expect you to enclose a stamped addressed envelope for the return of your unwanted material otherwise they may not return it. Be patient and do not expect a reply immediately; most editors are very busy people and are probably having to look at hundreds of pictures and slides every week.

With regard to payment most publishers have set rates of reproduction fees but some are by arrangement. Most publishers pay for reproduction use. The copyright in the picture remains yours. If a publisher wants to buy outright copyright or claims it, then be careful and make sure you get adequate payment. Payment of reproduction fees is only usually made on publication of material and not on acceptance.

If your material is accepted do not be discouraged if your pictures are not used immediately; features in magazines and books are planned well ahead and editors like to have a store of material from which to draw. Topical news pictures in contrast might find immediate use.

Joining photographic clubs

So much can be learnt about photography from joining a photographic club. There are always experienced photographers on hand who are prepared to spend time in helping newcomers to overcome their photographic problems. Photographic clubs and societies contain many fine photographers and one can only improve by looking at their work and also by finding out the technical details of the photographs. Most fair sized towns have a photographic club or society and details of them can usually be obtained at the local public library.

Another very useful thing, especially for beginners would be to enroll in a photographic course at the local night school. This is where you would be shown the basics of developing a black and white film and printing the negatives. Some courses also deal with colour work. Night school courses are advertised in the local press and details can be obtained at the night schools concerned. These courses are usually run by experienced photographers and are generally good value for money.

Reading Material

Read as many photographic books as you can. You can always benefit from learning about the top photographers' style and technique.

Also there are weekly and monthly magazines like *Amateur Photographer* and *Practical Photography,* all of which abound in excellent tips and hints on all facets of photography, and of course there are many quality illustrated railway books and magazines.

Photographing abroad

Many railway photographers now travel overseas to see and photograph the railways of the world, particularly to the countries where steam locomotives are still used in any numbers. But whether you are travelling just across the water to France or as far afield as Africa, South America or the Far East, there are certain points worth bearing in mind.

Although film can be obtained in most countries and in one or two places it may even be cheaper, it certainly pays to take enough with you thus avoiding any problems that may arise. Processing can also be difficult abroad so it is preferable to have your films processed when you get home.

Avoid letting your film, whether exposed or unexposed go through airport X-ray checks. No matter what people say there is always a chance of the X-ray ruining your film and in consequence one of the main purposes of your holiday. Keep all your film separate from your cameras and ask for the film to be checked by hand. This may mean rewinding the film in your camera that may have only been half exposed but could be well worth it in the long run. If you are using 120 size film you will lose a few frames but with 35mm it is possible to use the rest of the film again. Before rewinding make a note of the exposures taken and then rewind but not completely into the cassette. There is a slight clicking sound as the film comes off the spool and if you stop at that juncture the film leader will still be out of the cassette thus enabling you to load the film again.

To reload the film in the camera load the film leader in the take up spool, as normal, and close the back of the camera. *Then most important of all place the lens cap on the lens thus making the camera light tight.* Then taking a note of the frames already exposed, say 16, shoot off 19 exposures (*with the cap still on the lens*). You will then be ready to expose the film in the normal way, having wasted only two or three exposures.

If possible always take a spare camera with you, for if your camera does break down the chances of getting it repaired are extremely remote, especially in some of the more

A Class 40 threads Princess Street Gardens, Edinburgh with a train from the north of Scotland, 19 June 1966. Side lighting has helped to create strong contrasting highlights but great care was taken with exposure to retain detail in the shadow area. This was achieved by taking a light reading for both the shadow and highlight areas and using a balance of the two readings. Highlights were given extra exposure at the printing stage. Note the fine architecture of the building in the background and how it balances the picture.

Camera, Konica range-finder with 45mm plus yellow filter. Exposure 1/250th sec at f5·6. Film, Kodak Plus X (rated at 125ASA), developed in D 76 (undiluted).

exotic places that railway photographers get to.

Extremes of temperature can affect cameras and films. In very cold icy weather the camera shutter can be adversely affected and if you are photographing in such conditions keep your camera warm by carrying it inside a case or bag, only removing the camera just before taking a shot and then putting it away as soon as possible.

Film can be affected by hot humid conditions as well as cold weather so keep all film (when not in your camera) in plastic containers. This will certainly help to cut down on the damage that may be done by very adverse weather conditions.

Finally remember that not all countries accept that railway photographers are carrying out a harmless hobby. In a few extremes, even steam locomotives are among state property to be kept secret, and photographing them is tantamount

to spying. Thus official permits might be required even if photographing at stations. On British Rail you may take photographs anywhere where the public is normally permitted at stations – with a ticket if necessary. Sheds, depots and other railway property require a permit from the Regional Public Relations Officer concerned on BR, or from the General Managers of the individual private railways.

A Birmingham to Wolverhampton EMU pulls out of Tipton on 1 July 1982 and passes a narrow boat on the Birmingham Canal. Note the contrast in modes of transport and how the picture is framed by the overbridge and also how the reflections in the canal give depth to an otherwise elongated image. The verticals here are tricky since the bridge pier is not upright, the catenary masts are, and train is on a canted curve.

Camera, Nikon FM with 50mm lens plus yellow filter. Exposure 1/500th sec at f5·6. Film, Ilford XP1 (rated at 400ASA), developed in XP1 chemicals.

10
Steam Portfolio

On a murky day at the end of winter LMS Pacific No 6201 *Princess Elizabeth* climbs out of Shrewsbury with a south-bound Welsh Marches Pullman. The location is Baystone Hill and the date 20 March 1982. This classic pictorial approach shows an engine taken at the moment that the buffer beam intersects the line between the fence posts on the

left and the base of the tree on the right, so that the chimney falls on the Golden Section. The structure relies on tri-angles, such as the one formed by the track leading to the bend (left,) then returning up through the meadow (right,) and the top of the tree. Another one is formed by the same track and bend, but including the height of the

exhaust. The beauty of this locomotive is greatly enhanced by the way the oak tree on the right echoes the billowing steam.

Camera, Nikon FM with 50mm lens plus yellow filter. Exposure 1/500th sec at f4·5. Film, Ilford XP1 (rated at 400ASA), developed in XP1 chemicals.

Patrick Stirling's 8ft single 4–2–2 No 1 of 1870 makes a fine sight as it storms out of Loughborough on the Great Central Railway with a train for Rothley.

This beautiful engine was on temporary loan from the National Railway Museum at York. By enclosing the train in a cutting, flanked by tall trees, and by taking the engine nearly head-on with a 135mm lens, I succeeded in conveying the effect of compressed power. This is helped by a low viewpoint and a vertical format, which shows the towering exhaust to greater advantage. As I took this picture on the shadow side, I allowed half a stop overexposure. This coupled with the reflected light off the ballast gave some detail in the shadows, which were brought out in the printing stage. 13 June 1982.

Camera, Nikon FM with 135mm lens plus yellow filter. Exposure 1/500th sec at f6·3. Film, Ilford FP4 (rated at 200ASA), developed in Acuspecial.

Another beautiful vintage locomotive, *Maude*, a North British Railway 0–6–0 of 1888, poses for the camera at Blackburn station on the evening of 17 May 1980. It was on its way from the Scottish Railway Preservation Society at Falkirk to Rainhill for the Liverpool & Manchester 150th anniversary celebrations. I caught sight of the locomotive waiting for a path, and recognised at once the potential of the scene. This relies on the repeating rhythms of the arches in the wall and the circular forms in the engine, such as the wheels, the dome, the name and headboard, and the banding on the boiler. This is definitely a picture for black and white film, and shows up the gloss of the paintwork against the texture of the sooty stone walls and the pattern of the rails. The four intervening tracks are compressed by the use of a short telephoto lens. The finishing touch comes from the jet of white steam which relieves the blackness. Notice how the focus of interest, ie the driver and fireman, falls on the Golden Section and how the raised forearm follows into the curve of the left-hand arch.

Camera, Nikon FM with 85mm lens plus yellow filter. Exposure 1/250th second at f5·6. Film, Ilford FP4 (rated at 160ASA), developed in Aculux.

South African Railways Class 25 4–8–4 No 3515 climbs into Sheridan with the 0745 (Saturdays only) Bethlehem–Ficksburg on 24 July 1982, midwinter in the southern hemisphere. In previous years this view had not been attractive because of the clutter of maize stalks, but since the field had been drilled for grass, this seemed an ideal opportunity to use the ribbed surface as a foreground with character. This layered construction enabled me to raise the subject to the upper Golden Section, and its proportions let me take in the whole of the train. The tree behind the guard's van is very important as a counter balance to the visual weight of the engine, and it forms the other footing for the arch of steam in the sky.

Camera, Nikon FM with 50mm lens plus yellow filter. Exposure 1/250th second at f5·6. Film, Ilford Pan F (50ASA), developed in I D11 (undiluted).

Portuguese Railways 4–6–0 No 291 (built by Henschel in 1913) crosses the junction of the River Tua and River Douro at Tua with a morning train from Regua bound for Barca D'Alva (near the Spanish border), 23 September 1974.

The locomotive here is a little above the Golden Section, but it was very important to include the foot of the pier where it met the river. In any case, the masonry columns looked so heavy that it was visually necessary to lift them clear of the bottom edge. These strongly contrasting features counterbalance the other three-quarters of the composition, which clearly show the fine variations in plant forms clinging to the mountain slopes. Some dramatic ten-

sion is developed by including the group of men using the catwalk as the engine approaches.

Camera, Nikkormat with 85mm lens plus yellow filter. Exposure 1/500th sec at f8. Film, Ilford FP4 (rated at 200ASA), developed in Acuspecial.

On a lovely Autumn day, Midland compound 4–4–0 No 1000 speeds south out of Harrogate with a special York circular train chartered by the Ford Motor Company. The date 7 October 1981.

In this picture, the setting breaks down into distinct areas of texture, such as the willow herb in the lower left hand corner, and their middle greys make a perfect foil for the light and dark of the locomotive. The use of a yellow filter makes sure that the green trees in the cutting become light enough to make the darker locomotive stand out. Notice how the front of the boiler is further accentuated by catching it as it crosses a sunny patch of dry grass. A high viewpoint gives the track a dynamic diagonal slope. The engine is counterbalanced by the bridge and church steeple glimpsed through the trees.

Camera, Nikon FM with 50mm lens plus yellow filter. Exposure 1/500th sec at f8. Film, Ilford XP1 (400ASA) developed in XP1 chemicals.

Isle of Man Railway 2–4–0 *Loch* pulls out of Douglas station on 31 August 1974 with the 2.15 pm to Port Erin.

Notice how the line of the slope of the roof continues through the tilted cap of the driver and down to the object of his attention – the jet of steam from the cylinder cocks. The same line continues to the points lever on the left. This scene captures the holiday spirit in the faces of the children on the right, eagerly watching the track ahead. The characteristic feature of these engines, the highly-polished brass dome, stands out clearly against a background of darker foliage.

Camera, Nikkormat with 35mm lens plus yellow filter. Exposure 1/500th sec at f6·3. Film, Ilford FP4 (rated at 200ASA), developed in Acuspecial.

On the picturesque George–Knysna branch in Cape Province, South African Railways Class 24 2–8–4 No 3652 is caught in a silhouette pose as it crosses the lakes near Rondevlei with the mid-day George–Knysna train. To obtain this shot I filmed from inside the car to shelter the lens from the direct glare of the sun. Whenever there is no detail visible on the engine because it is in silhouette, there should be compensating interest in the surrounding areas. These mudflats on the borders of the lagoon break up the water into a sparkling texture, reflecting the direct morning sunlight. I chose this spot to park the car as the hills rose up into a conspicuous summit at this point, and the only cloud in the sky fitted in very nicely above it. Although the causeway was level, I knew the engine would be working reasonably hard and the exhaust that I expected would show up clearly against the darker hills.

Camera, Nikon FM with 50mm lens plus yellow filter. Exposure 1/500th sec at f8. Film, Ilford FP4 (rated at 200ASA), developed in Acuspecial.

24 February 1981. Wolkenstein, East Germany. No 991 585, a Meyer 0–4–4–0 tank (75cm gauge) shunts in the station yard. This example of the 'starburst' structure shows the lines of perspective continuing invisibly from the top and bottom of the building and from the carriage on the left, towards the chimney of the locomotive. The confined space frames it perfectly. It was a bitterly cold day as can be seen from the exhaust, and the stark black shape of the building with its broken gutter accentuates the mood, as do the smashed windows at the left. This scene is made even more dramatic by the glimpses round the corner, reflected in the carriage.

Camera, Nikon FM with 50mm lens plus yellow filter. Exposure 1/250th sec at f4. Film, Ilford FP4 (rated at 160ASA), developed in Aculux.

Midland compound 4–4–0 No 1000 poses at Carlisle Upperby on a bitterly cold winter's night, 11 February 1983.

This classic three-quarter front portrait is given greater power and elegance by the low viewpoint of the camera on a tripod. The boiler towers over the photographer, rising in dynamic diagonals, while the lens being closer to the ground picks out the details of the wheels. This low angle also makes the locomotive cover up any unwanted poles that otherwise would spoil the profile.

The lighting conditions were most exciting – and demanding – as it was very dark, the only sources of illumination being the lamp behind the boiler and the gleam of snow. As the locomotive was a black silhouette, I had to use about five fill-in flashes along the side and three from one spot at the front to build up more light.

Camera, Nikon FM with 35mm lens. Exposure, 1½ min. at f8 with fill-in flash. Film, Ilford XP1 rated at 400ASA and developed in XP1 chemicals.

25 February 1968. Lostock Hall shed Preston. Class 5 4–6–0 No 45345 receives admiring glances before moving off shed to Preston station to work out the 17·52 to Liverpool.

Here is an example of the exception proving the rule where the golden section has been abandoned in favour of a dramatic imbalance. This increases the massive size of the locomotive against the tiny figures of the photographers. Notice how important is the man's raised arm which follows the diagonal structure.

Camera, Konica rangefinder with 45mm lens and yellow filter. Exposure 1/125th sec at f8. Film, Kodak Plus X rated at 125ASA developed in D76 (undiluted).

Veteran 0–6–0 *Maude* hurries through Princess Street Gardens Edinburgh on the 4 May 1980 with a special to Inverkeithing.

This charming setting for an historic locomotive shows railway photography in its most delightful aspect. The fresh budding branches form a perfect foil for the white exhaust, and while the treetrunks do grow out of the engine, they form such a consistent pattern that the eye accepts them as a texture. I only had to be careful to catch the chimney in a clear space. A few dark twigs in the top corner help to round off the picture and balance the darker engine.

The raised viewpoint makes the rails slope more steeply and lends a sense of impatience as *Maude* gathers speed.

The other diagonal comes from the steam, making an arrowhead shape with the track.

Camera, Nikkormat with 50mm standard lens plus yellow filter. Exposure, 1/250th sec at f4·5. Film, Ilford FP4 rated at 160ASA developed in Aculux.

Cadley Hill Colliery near Burton on Trent. *Cadley Hill No 1* a Hunslet 0–6–0 shunts at the exchange sidings. 25 May 1972.

A warm day with diffuse lighting and with little exhaust showing presents a challenge to every photographer. Fortunately I spotted this pattern of siding points which echoed the curve of the saddletank, and by using a high viewpoint and medium telephoto lens I was able to make the tracks play an important part in this composition.

Camera, Nikkormat with 135mm lens plus yellow filter. Exposure, 1/250th second at f8. Film, Ilford FP4 rated at 200ASA developed in Acuspecial.

60009 *Union of South Africa* storms up to Plean Junction south of Stirling with an Ediburgh-Aberdeen special. 18 April 1981.

Sunlight from behind throws up the exhaust with dramatic edgelighting against a pale sky, and renders the two subjects almost as silhouettes. The effect of compressed power is increased by using a short telephoto lens to bunch-up slightly the perspective of the coaches. Notice how the slope of the semaphore leads the to the chimney of the locomotive, which although it is near the centre of the composition, is visually drawn to the right by the signals.

Camera, Nikon FM with 85mm lens plus yellow filter. Exposure, 1/500th sec at f6·3. Film, Ilford FP4 rated at 160ASA developed in Aculux.

Glossary

Aperture
This is the circular opening with a camera lens that controls the amount of light reaching the film. The size of the lens opening is indicated by the f number. The higher the f number the smaller the opening and therefore less light. The lower the f number the wider the opening and more light striking the film. Each higher full aperture f number allows half the light of its adjacent lower number; f11 is half of f8, f16 is half f11, etc.

ASA
This is the term used to indicate the speed of films. The lower the number the slower the film and the higher the number the faster the film.

In practical terms if you were using a 50 ASA film which gave you a shutter speed of 125th second at f5·6 the equivalent exposure if using 100 ASA film would be 125th second at f8 or 250th second at f5·6. So therefore 100 ASA film is twice as fast as 50 ASA and 200 ASA is twice as fast as 100 ASA etc.

Average metering
This is when meter readings of the whole scene are taken and evaluated to assess the exposure.

'B'
Shutter speed setting at which the shutter will remain open as long as the release is held down.

Compact camera
Small 35mm camera with a fixed lens.

Depth of field
Depth of field is the distance between the nearest and furthest points of the subject which are ac-ceptably sharp. It increases with the higher aperture f numbers, and decreases with the lower f numbers.

DIN
This is the continental system for indicating the speed of films (see ASA above) but the numbers differ from ASA numbers and below are the main equivalent speeds.

15 DIN	=	25 ASA
18 DIN	=	50 ASA
19 DIN	=	64 ASA
21 DIN	=	100 ASA
22 DIN	=	125 ASA
24 DIN	=	200 ASA
27 DIN	=	400 ASA

Exposure
This is the total amount of light which reaches the film and is controlled by the lens aperture and shutter speed.

Film speed
The sensitivity of a film to light. This is usually measured in the terms of ASA or DIN numbers. The lower the number the slower the film and the higher the number the faster the film.

Filter
A glass or synthetic lens attachment used to alter the quality and amount of light passing through a lens.

f number
This is used to measure the aperture (opening) of the lens. Low numbers represent wide apertures and high numbers represent smaller apertures, usually in the progression f2·8, f4, f5·6, f8, f11, f16, f22.

Focal length
The focal length of any lens is the distance between the rear nodal point of the lens and the focal plane (film plane) when the lens is focused on infinity.

Hot shoe
A camera fitting accessory on which to fit a flash gun. In this position by a contact on the hot shoe the flash unit will fire when the camera shutter is fired.

Light meter
A device for measuring light, to aid the determination of correct exposure.

Reciprocity failure
A normal light meter gives accurate readings, with alternative equivalent settings for shutter and aperture in the daylight range of illumination. But in very dark conditions these equivalents fall out of step, and the meter cannot be relied upon for long exposures.

Self timer
This mechanical or electronic device delays the firing of the shutter for up to 10 seconds after the photographer has pressed the shutter release. Very useful for taking self portraits with your favourite locomotive.

Shutter
Camera mechanism controlling the length of exposure.

Shutter speed
Length of time which the shutter is open during exposure.

SLR
Single lens reflex camera in which the photographer looks directly through the taking lens.

Standard lens
Camera lens of a focal length approximating to the diagonal of the negative format. Also a lens which produces the most natural perspective image in relation to the picture area.

Telephoto lens
This is a lens with a focal length greater than that of a standard lens.

TLR
Twin lens reflex camera. This camera is fitted with two lenses (of the same focal length) coupled together, one for taking the picture, the other for viewing and focusing.

TTL
This simply means through the lens. Thus we get TTL metering (metering through the lens) etc.

Wide angle lens
Lens with focal length less than a standard lens.

Zoom lens
Lens with variable focal length.

Index

First published in Great Britain in 1983 by
David & Charles (Publishers) Limited
under the title *A Handbook of Railway Photography*

This edition published in 1989 by
Peerage Books
Michelin House
81 Fulham Road
London SW3 6RB

ISBN 1 85052 133 6

Produced by Mandarin Offset
Printed and bound in Hong Kong